What Others Sa

In retelling Bible stories we thought we knew, Lee Van Ham demonstrates how scandal and subterfuge lay the groundwork for a "compelling" new incarnation story and a sorely needed new creation for the earth. Some of its elements: the vision of economic equality articulated by the Virgin Mary, the acceptance of immigrants, ethnic minorities, outcasts, and women by Jesus and his disciples, the celebration of the divine in all of us and in all things. To embrace this vision, we must see with new eyes, must find our lost capacity for awe. Excavated from ancient Hebrew stories and the "radical good news" of the Gospels of Matthew and Luke, here is a path to spiritual transformation—both personal and communal—for the times in which we find ourselves. Come and see for yourself.

— Deborah E. Ryel, poet, Associate Professor
of English, College of Dupage, Illinois

Speaking in a moment in history where Western politics, culture, and church are more and more supportive of imperial-driven, empire-seeking, and capital-centric ways of being, Van Ham's re-framing of Jesus' birth-story sheds a much-needed light on not only the destructive nature of the traditional Christmas story but also on the true nature of the gospel. When the Church's scriptures and creeds are ones birthed out of the imperial church rather than the Way of Jesus, it is necessary to dive deeper into the truly transformational gospel stories that continually show that the true gospel is one that can only be lived out through using a OneEarth theology. We must take on the true meaning of *ekklesia* and "call out" the harmful practices of the current MultiEarth Church and its harmful message in favor of one that puts Mother Earth and the OneEarth gospel of Jesus at the centre. Van Ham's message is clear: the earth cannot support humanity unless we shift from a MultiEarth understanding of scripture and Jesus's birth, to a OneEarth understanding.

— Emo Yango, Program Coordinator, Discipleship
and Witness (United Church of Canada); Strategic
Associate (Canadian Baptist Ministries)

What do economics, ecology, and Christmas have to do with one another? How did we miss Mary, the mother of Jesus, gift to us (to the world) as an economist? Read on. But beware, this is one of those books that will comfort the disturbed and disturb the comfortable. Lee Van Ham communicates from both mind and heart the significance of reclaiming the story of the birth of Jesus. A great book to buy for your church or to use to start a book club within your church or community. Van Ham offers a hopeful invitation to re-imagine the way we live. I highly recommend this book!"

— Mike Little, Director of Faith & Money Network, Washington, D.C.

Lee Van Ham has given the world a precious healing Christmas gift, recovering and retelling the One Earth birth story of Jesus as an alternative to the destructive Multi-Earth gluttony of gifts of our modern commercialized Christmas. Using the wisdom and lived experiences of the women of Jesus's family, Van Ham unearths a call for radical redistribution of the abundance of God to all. Read this book, and share it with your loved ones at this year's holiday table.

— Scott Klinger, Senior Equitable Development Specialist, Jobs with Justice

Lee Van Ham's book *The Liberating Birth of Jesus: A Birth Story Able to Reverse Our Planet's Perils*, is a survival narrative, not just for the Christian and spiritual among us, but for those of us tired of the MultiEarth story. He reminds us of the important distinctions between Christ and Jesus, the man, and how we can be part of this humble, cooperative theology. This is more than a 'Christmas story,' and is a powerful reframing of theology as one part of Mother Earth's beautiful history.

— Rachel Miller-Haughton, Fulbright Mexico Grantee in 2017

Reader beware!
Those blessed by a walk or swift swim…,
a skate on ice…, a view of a mountain rim…
delight in this "not-a-minute-too-early page turner".
Those who haven't: You, too: Beware!
You, too, as you do read, may just "catch the bug"
and decide to toss "multi-Earth ways" under the rug….
then live free— as a "Mother Earth" lover and learner.

— Ilse Meyer, M.A.English, Kiel Univ., Germany; M.A. German, U.C. Berkeley

For an exciting, new and refreshing account of the birth of Jesus—and its significance in this perilous time for the survival of our planet, look no further than Lee Van Ham's latest book, "The Liberating Birth of Jesus." Based on the infancy narratives of the Gospels of Matthew and Luke, Van Ham's thorough exegesis takes the reader all the way back to the Genesis story and to Jesus' genealogy that includes four "outsider" women (Rahab, Tamar, Ruth, Bathsheba) and thereby distances itself from the royal, official line of descent for the infant Jesus. Here is "newness"!

Van Ham "mines" every detail of the beloved, well-memorized Christmas story. At each step of Matthew's & Luke's narratives—involving the whole lineup of Elizabeth, Zechariah, Mary, Joseph, Simeon, Anna, the Magi, plus the "heavenly host" of angels proclaiming the "good news" to the shepherds... and the birth of Jesus himself —the author shows the "newness" of these events. Jesus' birth is grand in its humility! Likewise, it is NOT part of the ruling economic structure of societies that "go for the money" and eventually seek a "multi-earth" rather than a "one-earth" economy. In contrast, "OneEarth Economy" respects both the abundance of nature and the limits necessary to preserve its balance. There is true excitement in Van Ham's unveiling of this truth as he re-tells the familiar Christmas story.

In addition to respecting Van Ham's solid Biblical scholarship, I found myself deeply moved by his sensitive presentation of the pre-birth narratives of both Mary and Elizabeth.

— Daniel P. Meyer, PhD Theology, Gregorian University in Rome

If as a Christian you have had any dis-ease around the celebration of Christmas, this book offers some of why that is. Additionally it offers insight as to where the good news of the coming of the Christ can lead us in our current desperate circumstances. We must accept the challenge of one-earth living.

— Paul Taylor, businessman and Board President of Faith & Money Network

Read this book and you will never experience Christmas the same way again. Lee Van Ham shows how Christ's birth was meant to signal a new creation with deep implications for care for the earth and for each other. That surely calls for celebration, but not the one we're used to.

— William Dyrness, Senior Professor of Theology and Culture, Fuller Theological Seminary, Pasadena, California

THE LIBERATING BIRTH OF JESUS

Other Books and Articles by the Author

Jubilee Circles: Helping Save Life on the Planet
2017, co-authored with Richard Lawrence, OneEarth Publishing.

From Egos to Eden: Our Heroic Journey to Keep Earth Livable
2016, OneEarth Publishing.

Blinded by Progress: Breaking Out of the Illusion That Holds Us
2013, OneEarth Publishing. A Korean edition was published
in 2015 by Jeeyoungsa Publishing, Seoul, Korea.

*"Unmasking the Gods of the Marketplace," a chapter
in Nurturing the Prophetic Imagination*
Wipf & Stock, (2012)

The
Liberating
Birth of Jesus

A Birth Story Able to Reverse Our Planet's Perils

Lee Van Ham

OneEarth Publishing
SAN DIEGO, CALIFORNIA

The Liberating Birth of Jesus:
A Birth Story Able to Reverse Our Planet's Perils
© 2019, Lee Van Ham. All Rights Reserved.
Published by OneEarth Publishing, San Diego, California

ISBN 978-1-7340299-0-1 (paperback)
ISBN 978-1-7340299-1-8 (eBook)

http://theoneearthproject.com/

Indexing by Catherine Barr
Publishing consultant: David Wogahn, AuthorImprints.com

Contents

Notes to Readers on How I Use Terms in This Book

Cosmology combines science, mystery, and spirit. It dwarfs empires and human history. It's unruly in that empires cannot control it, and that's what also makes it paradigm-altering. Cosmology transcends the dualism of seeing reality as the earth and the heavens. Both are part of a large whole, the cosmos.

Creation-centered thinking and living means that nature's genius is a primary authority in our lives—more than money, advanced degrees, religious tradition, political party, ego, and other centers of authority.

Empire is a concept of governing that exercises power over others and enforces such control through laws, police, and military strength. Empires seek technological and industrial superiority over other regions. The system of government may be totalitarian with dictators in charge, but can also be various forms of democracy. Nature is there for the benefit and profit of the empire.

MultiEarth names a way of thinking, living, and shaping societies that requires the capacities of more than our planet. **OneEarth** names a contrasting way of thinking, living, and shaping societies that requires no more than Earth's abundant capacities.

New Creation is the sense that because of an event, our way of understanding everything has changed. What wasn't possible, becomes possible. The way we had seen and understood the world becomes obsolete. The world as understood in the greater consciousness of the soul (also Christ consciousness) differs night to day from the world as understood with the consciousness of our egos.

Panentheism is a more comprehensive way to think about God than either theism or pantheism. Not only is God in every cell, but also in every process and interaction. God is not "out there," but here, within, and among. The fullness of this mystery is further revealed when we add that all that is and happens are in God as well. Shifting to such thinking has become essential for the survival of life.

Soul is the English word for the Greek word "psyche," the root for the word psychology. Though some consider soul to be a word to use when talking about spirituality and psyche more for use in matters scientific, for me the words are largely equivalent. The soul includes the realm of the unconscious, a larger center of identity than what ego can provide. Our souls also have the tools to connect with mystery, the Divine, and cosmology.

Wild names all that is outside of what a society deems normal, or even moral. What is wild to the MultiEarth way of controlling the world is liberating for people committed to OneEarth living. There is a sense of sovereignty and interdependence in the wild that threatens MultiEarth ways. Wildness is necessary for fuller development of our humanness.

Foreword

"PEACEWEAVINGS" WAS THE NAME CHOSEN for the intentional community we established in Chicago in 2000. Lee Van Ham was guiding our discussion when the name was agreed upon by consensus. From that day forward, I have known Lee to be 'weaving peace' in ever expanding, deeper, more provocative ways. After leaving the parish ministry in suburbia Chicago in 1999, Lee and his wife Juanita moved into Chicago responding with others to an invitation to live communally and more sustainably. The birthing of Peaceweavings quickly developed into the recognition that making peace has broader meanings than just resolving differences between discordant factions.

Leading up to forming Peaceweavings, my husband, Tom, and I were asked by friends, Ross and Gloria Kinsler, to read the manuscript of what would become their book, *The Biblical Jubilee and the Struggle for Life*. Accordingly, we asked those considering living intentionally in community to read it also. There we were challenged to explore the biblical vision of jubilee. As we worked through the implications of comunal living, it became apparent that the biblical jubilee stands in sharp contrast to the individualistic, competitive undergirding of our capitalist economic system. In addition to Peaceweavings, we formed a nonprofit, Jubilee Economics Ministries, to present the jubilee vision and practice in the 21st century.

Health issues moved Lee and Juanita to San Diego, California, but Lee's continuing probe into living out the commonwealth of jubilee never abated. Jubilee Economics Ministries expanded to include communities in Mexico, thus incorporating a much needed developing world perspective. Lee's scholarship led him into an ever-expanding exploration to connect jubilee with the climate crisis underway, which in large part is growing out of our human determination to use an economic model that extracts from God's good creation wealth meant for all, but benefitting the exclusive few. Thus the OneEarth project was born, meaning that we must learn to live within the capacities of the one Earth we have. Obsessed by the catastrophic changes occurring in our planet, Lee has written extensively about the call to humanity to not only become aware, but also make very difficult decisions to change our self-interested life styles, to weave peace into the very web of life. See his books, *Blinded by Progress* (2013) and *From Egos to Eden* (2016).

In this new book, *The Liberating Birth of Jesus,* Lee weaves the birth of Jesus narratives into an illustration of how we can reverse the current ecological catastrophe within a new creation story. He aptly includes specific ways we must stand with Mother Earth to realize the goal of OneEarth living through spiritual activism. In making reference to Jesus' ancestors, Lee leads us in exposing MultiEarth and empire complexes, making them obsolete. Expect to be surprised, challenged and encouraged by this soul-searching, provocative journey from Peaceweavings to OneEarth living.

Grace Gyori

2019

CHAPTER ONE

Liberating the Birth of Jesus from Christmas

Jesus' Birth and Christmas: Two Different Stories

The birth story told in the gospels is nothing like the Christmas story told in the shopping malls of the world—or even the story told in most churches. From Black Friday sales on, Christmas comes in a parade of clever ads: "Buy, and get into the spirit of giving." Lights twinkle magically day and night. Homes are adorned with favorite decorations. Families renew holiday traditions. Church observances attract more people than usual.

By contrast, the gospels tell a story with the power to effect deep change. People changed economic practices and leveled inequities. Hierarchies based on race and class gave way to arrangements that facilitated cooperation and sharing. Political understandings of power as control and domination yielded to sharing power among all so that right relationships prevailed. And spirituality moved out of the institutions of religion and the clutches of professional practitioners into nature, the streets, and homes. There the Spirit constantly regenerated life marked by a liberating justice. Ever so eloquently and boldly, the

Gospels tell a story of a new creation. That story gave its contemporaries a compelling and more just alternative to the story proclaimed by the Roman Empire and the other powers of the time.

It follows, then, that it is for us to take the story of the Gospels and tell it compellingly in our time. To tell it in ways that we counter the overwhelming breakdowns across Earth's ecological systems, and that heal humanity's separation from creation and our divisions shaped according to skin color, those who have and those who don't, and the collapse of compassion. Making that story of a new creation compelling in our world today is the purpose of this book.

Conflicted and Restless at Christmastime

For years I've been restless about Christmas. At times I've really loved it. But it's also been a burden and has left my soul empty. Sometimes I've found some of its magic—usually with children or a tree that becomes the Tree of Life for me. But I've rarely felt that the full power of the birth story given in the Gospels was being released during the Christmas season. What I realize now is that I was trying to merge the Christmas story with the birth story. But it hasn't worked because the stories exist in two different worldviews, and the two cannot be merged successfully. Depending on which worldview we use, we think about the world differently and each shapes our lives differently. In many basic ways, the worldviews are actually opposed to one another. Instead of trying to merge them, I've come to realize that I need to choose between them.

My earnest effort to fit the story of the birth of Jesus into the worldview that shapes Christmas, left me deeply dissatisfied. The birth story lost out. I watched the raw, cosmic, wildness of the Gospels evaporate in Christmas dramas and pageantry. Every year, the magi's gifts get translated into "Christmas is a time of giving." The trans-forming moments of the journey of the magi, and the significance of their gift-giving, get lost in wrappings and ribbons of thousands of purchases. There's no hint that this birth is about the new creation essential to the livability and sustainability of our planet today.

I've come to realize that the restlessness I've experienced about Christmas is due to not recognizing that the story in the Gospels had been taken captive by "Christian" cultures. What Matthew and Luke put forth in their Gospels lifted people into a new consciousness and empowered new structures that broke down barriers of class and race, democratized political power, and exposed the injustices of imperial economics. Powerful alternatives were created. But when the birth came to be celebrated in the imperial church, the liturgies and fes-tivals tamed the story enough that its transforming powers faltered. Many of those liturgies and festivals are beautiful; and celebrations in various cultures have added their own interpretations and symbols over the years. But the power of change has dwindled. It doesn't have the spiritual force equal to the massive mobilization for change that is essential now.

For the 32 years that I pastored three different congregations I did my best to create beautiful, moving experiences for all who attended special worship on Christmas Eve. Many love candlelight services, the special music, and other elements, all of which involve lots of work from church staff and volunteers. A great deal of money is spent. Many are moved by these services and connect with the Holy. Yet, are peo-ple moved enough to make the changes that the gospels describe? Or alarmingly, that the Earth tells us are necessary today? At the time, I did not understand that the power of the story of Jesus' birth, as told by Matthew and Luke, is neutered when put into the structures of imperial religion or an economy and culture dedicated to living at levels of affluence beyond the capacities of the planet.

Then I made a discovery.

Discovery: The Two Stories Exist in Separate Worldviews

The Christmas story celebrated December 25 is not the story of the birth of Jesus as Matthew and Luke tell it. The two exist in different realms and worldviews. The Christmas story is in a worldview where the world is shaped by empires, by financial and business structures that dominate most humans and all the species of nature. The powers that be in this worldview are ego-driven and violate nature's systems, which evolved to sustain all of life. In this way of thinking, humans consider themselves above nature.

The birth of Jesus, on the other hand, is part of the worldview in which creation is the measure of life. Here humans consider themselves within nature, part of her systems of life. If embraced, humans live within this worldview from within a deeper and greater sense of who they are than only their egos. Living with this sense of soul, humans become more cooperative and sharing, less controlling, selfish, and bullying.

The birth of Jesus happened in Bethlehem, probably in 6 B.C.E. The Christmas story didn't begin taking shape until more than 300 years later. The birth of Jesus likely happened in the home of a peasant family, not in an ancient barn or stable as conventional wisdom has it. It was announced to shepherds out in the fields, in nature with their sheep. The Christmas story happened in a church after Constantine was emperor and had made "Christianity" the empire's official religion. The first recorded Christ Mass happened in 336 C.E. That's when Christmas was born. It didn't happen during the reign of Caesar Augustus, a solidly pagan Emperor who drew to himself notions of deity, but in the reign of Constantine, the first "Christian" emperor. Churches were far too ready to embrace his welcome to them despite that doing so rejected the non-imperial way of Jesus.

When I first discovered how two worldviews were vying for our hearts and minds, I didn't have Christmas on my mind. I was asking, "Why are we humans, who pride ourselves on being an intelligent species, shaping livestyles and economies that require more than the capacities of our planet?" I wanted to find answers beyond the usual, beyond those who said, "We're too greedy." Or, "It's the human condition." I began writing because it disciplined me to research and articulate the relevant issues. Before long I began to see that there are basically two broad-based worldviews guiding life—one living with the planet's generosity, the other exceeding it. After casting about for names, I settled on *OneEarth* and *MultiEarth*—since it takes more than one planet to fulfill the material needs of the latter. To me, they clearly distinguish between the worldview that fits the planet and its limits and the one that exceeds them.

As I arrived at the names for these worldviews, I became aware of another author, Wes Howard-Brook, who teaches at the University of Seattle and has been working longer than I have on creating awareness of the two worldviews. He uses the names "empire religion" and "creation religion" which closely parallel MultiEarth and OneEarth, respectively. Among his books, the two that have especially influenced me are *"Come Out My People," God's Call Out of Empire in the Bible and Beyond* and *Empire Baptized: How the Church Embraced What Jesus Rejected.*

In these books Howard-Brook demonstrates how these two worldviews are in tension throughout the Bible and in the early centuries after Jesus. He shows how the followers of the Way of Jesus were replaced by a church shaped by imperial ways. As the subtitle of his book *Empire Baptized* says: The church embraced what Jesus rejected.

The tension between these worldviews still defines life in the here and now. Today, the Earth and her species are screaming out that living by the MultiEarth worldview (or empire religion) has devastating consequences for life on our planet. Though the Earth has absorbed some of the excesses of MultiEarth living over millennia, we have reached the tipping point. The Earth can no longer absorb MultiEarth excesses. Continuing to live in MultiEarth ways poses an existential threat to human life as well as to all other species.

The seeds for our contemporary predicament were sown when humans began the *Civilization Project*—a project consisting of agriculture, city life, trade, finance, and all that was part of the Neolithic (New Stone Age) Revolution beginning about 10,000 B.C.E. No one living then could have imagined how their choices would lead to what we face today. But the lineage of MultiEarth living follows a trajectory from that time to now.

Today, every decision needs to be weighed by this scale: "Does it serve MultiEarth or OneEarth ways?" Greening MultiEarth won't do. We must make Earth-size changes by 2030. That date has been set by the 2018 report of the UN's Intergovernmental Panel on Climate Change, a collective of thousands of scientists and other experts on the topic. The report warns that 2030 is our deadline to avoid massive erosion to Earth's livability for humans and all species.

I've continued to think about life in terms of MultiEarth and OneEarth, bringing all aspects of my life under a new scrutiny. Christmas is no exception. And that's what moved me to write this book. I wanted to look at Christmas in the light of these two worldviews. In doing so, I came to realize that the birth of Jesus in the Gospels has fallen victim to MultiEarth civilization. MultiEarth disheartens those of us working for OneEarth ways of life by taking captive many alternatives and revising them to serve its own purposes. This certainly happened when the lifeways Jesus intended were taken over by a church that shifted into the imperial paradigm.

It's like what happens frequently in small, green businesses. If a new business with potential for advancing OneEarth ways goes public instead and is on the stock markets, the founder may make a lot of money, but he or she loses control of what they started. Their efforts become part of a MultiEarth corporation. The potential to advance OneEarth ways is lost. That's the fate that befell the birth of Jesus in the Gospels when Christmas took it over.

The Birth of Christmas

Returning to early celebrations of Jesus' birth: There were none. Birth celebrations did not happen in the churches to which the apostle Paul wrote his letters, all within the decade of 50-60 C.E. (approximately). Any thought of actually celebrating the birth of Jesus was shunned by early Christian writers. Andrew McGowan, Dean and President of the Berkeley Divinity School at Yale, has written on the Biblical Archaeology Society website that

> There is no mention of birth celebrations in the writings of early Christian writers such as Irenaeus (c. 130–200) or Tertullian (c. 160–225). Origen of Alexandria (c. 165–264) goes so far as to mock Roman celebrations of birth anniversaries, dismissing them as "pagan" practices—a strong indication that Jesus' birth was not marked with similar festivities at that place and time [Origen's homily on Leviticus

8]. As far as we can tell, Christmas was not celebrated at all at this point.[1]

No birth date? No celebration.

Another consequence of the hostility toward celebrating birth anniversaries in early Christian communities was that if a birth date for Jesus was known earlier, it was forgotten. No mention is made of a birth date until a Christian teacher in Egypt does so around 200 C.E. Even then no consensus gathered around one date. Various teachers and writers from different regions did not agree, and no celebrations happened until a given date came into general acceptance.

The first Christ Mass happened as a direct result of a major shift in the religious-political environment in the opening years of the 4th century. Constantine struggled with many antagonistic factions across the Roman Empire. He put down some with his army, but he recognized that religion could be a "glue" he needed to bring together the divided leaders and people. He chose Christianity. Or it could be said that Christianity chose him due to a story about a dream in which he was told, "In this sign conquer." The sign was the cross. The authenticity of the story and its interpretation are contested. And the thought of God authorizing imperial conquest with the sign of the cross violates all understandings of God that aren't wed to the imperial and MultiEarth paradigm. Nonetheless, during Constantine's reign Christianity changed from a sect in the eyes of the empire to the official religion. What a different context this was from Bethlehem!

Another development in Constantine's rule shows the immediate implications of the political-religious change. What is called the first ecumenical (universal) council of churches happened in 325 C.E.

---

1   https://www.biblicalarchaeology.org/daily/people-cultures-in-the-bible/jesus-historical-jesus/how-december-25-became-christmas/, accessed 4-22-2019.

How it happened countered absolutely the birth stories of Matthew and Luke. The bishops and other church leaders of the time were engaged in a religious struggle that echoed Constantine's political struggles for unity across the empire. Belief, theology, and practice varied enough that they were contentious and divisive. Constantine needed the bishops to be united in order to strengthen his own efforts for unity across the empire. This brought the bishops and emperor into a common purpose. So Constantine invited all 1800 bishops of the Empire to Nicaea, in what is today northwestern Turkey. Not all bishops attended, but Constantine gave them free travel and lodging as an incentive. In 325 C.E., he opened the council and stayed to attend. The nature of the Son of God was the primary contentious issue. A creed was voted on. Those opposing were demoted in status. The political nature of how the Nicene Creed came to be is readily discernible.

It's beyond any informed imagination that Jesus would appeal for unity or claim authority via a creed *that did not offend an empire*. He operated from the consciousness in which he was one with the Father in Heaven rather than the Father in Rome. His consciousness understood that he was also one with all creation—all being infused, incarnated with the Most High. The Nicene Creed operates from a different consciousness. It is a confession of the imperial church, not the followers of the Way of Jesus. As creeds go, this one is definitely acceptable to imperial ways because it doesn't talk about *the teachings of Jesus*. His teaching are anti-imperial. But at Nicaea and in subsequent variations, the creed addressed only his birth, his nature, and his death and resurrection. Empires can be okay with such a creed—especially when the purpose is to bring unity, not to foster dissent, or rebellion, or a call to live out of alternatives to the ways shaped by the empire.

Furthermore, when creeds interpret the death of Jesus as the means to save people from their sins, it reminds everyone of a neediness that requires higher powers. People who see themselves in this way more readily accept external authority and power such as imperialism. On the other hand, interpretations of the passion of Jesus that emphasize how he died at the hands of the empire are essential to the Way of Jesus. His passion and resurrection confirm for followers of this Way that powers greater than the empire are at work and, if given our allegiance, can save and liberate us from the restrictions that make us less than human. Not only can humans be liberated, but all creation can be freed and the wound of our separation from creation can be healed.

But the Nicene Creed offers nothing in that regard. It is difficult for me to imagine why it continues to be chanted and spoken in liturgies to this day. The pressing issues of today differ greatly from those challenging the churches of Rome's empire in the fourth century. Churches must now mobilize the people to live the Way of Jesus and express vigorous love for the Earth and all species in the face of ecological breakdown.

The Nicene Creed is thus, a sterling example of how an imperial church conquers and colonizes transformational stories that inspire the powerless. The story of the birth of Jesus excellently portrays this method well. In the Council of Nicaea and the Nicene Creed, the story is not destroyed. It is just completely tamed by the systems operated by the powers that be. They take it captive, raiding the oppressed of a story able to transform their consciousness and how they see themselves in the world. It becomes an endearing story of gentle, civil humans dutifully honoring their deity with elements of imagination and mystery that make it special and interesting, but it no longer transforms people and institutions.

It was within the context of Constantine and Nicaea that Christmas was born. The first Christ Mass happened 336 C.E. Again, following McGowan in the Biblical Archaeology Society article quoted above, the earliest mention of December 25 as Jesus' birthday comes from a mid-fourth-century Roman almanac that lists the deaths of various Christian bishops and martyrs. There reference is made to December 25, marking it as the date of *"natus Christus in Betleem Judeae*: Christ was born in Bethlehem of Judea."

Even with a date for the birth, celebrating a Christ Mass was not immediately embraced. It did not spread quickly or evenly. But where it was celebrated, Jesus' birth was shaped by the church of the empire. The evolution of the Christmas celebrations is a saga of considerable interest and ingenuity across the centuries. But it's a saga in which Matthew's and Luke's versions are misunderstood and miscommunicated. They strain to be transforming whenever they are captive to political and economic empires. Today, the empires take a particular shape in dominating corporations and superpowers. Over the centuries, church celebrations have largely followed the imperial story more closely than the story of the Way of Jesus.

As Christmas came to be celebrated around the world, many beautiful celebrations have evolved that release a festive spirit and bring people together. They take on important elements of the culture of the region where the celebration happens. With few exceptions, the celebrations fit into the political and economic story of the region. They are primarily colonized versions of the birth of Jesus, if Jesus is mentioned at all.

EVENTS IN SEQUENCE	
27 BCE	Caesar Augustus begins reign
6 BCE	Birth of Jesus
50-57 CE	Paul's letters
66-70 CE	Gospel of Mark is written
70 CE	Jerusalem and Temple destroyed by Rome
85 CE	Matthew and Luke write Gospels
306 CE	Constantine becomes emperor of Rome
323 CE	Christianity is made the Roman Empire's official religion
336 CE	First Christ Mass

The Birth and Creation Story We Need to Avoid Ecological Collapse

The beauty and good in Christmas will not keep the Earth livable beyond 2030. Christmas is impotent to foster the revolution needed in consciousness and action. The ecological emergencies underway need far more "voltage" of soul and cosmos. I'm impatient for the release of the revolutionary energies of the birth of Jesus. That's what led me to write this book. As fine as these celebrations are, we can't be satisfied with them. We need stories that empower us to full capacity as we address the breakdowns and disasters of our time. The breakdowns are caused by living like Rome, not like Jesus. Life doesn't stay the same when the authentic stories around the birth of Jesus are released to touch the American way of life—or any culture's way of life. But filtered through the Christmas story, the revolution goes away.

As ecological disasters come to our attention daily, we need stories with the energies to revolutionize our thinking and practice. Furthermore, we need those stories now. The story of superpowers is killing us. Scientific reports continue to express alarm at the rapid rate of changes underway—destabilizing changes as greenhouse gases continue to increase in the atmosphere with the result that ice at the poles melts rapidly, coral reefs and marine life die, and species lose habitat to migrating seasons and irregular patterns of rainfall. Species are tumbling into extinction to the point where we cannot even estimate the impacts of such loss on the interdependent web of life. Speaking with the voices of prophets, scientists tell us that 1,000,000 species of plants and animals are likely to be gone in a few years. In geological time, it's like the blink of an eye. Humans are now included among the species threatened in this century.

The dead end of this all-too-prominent story can be explained by many elements. But at the heart, the life-support structures of civilization's story have evolved to require more than one planet to meet its demands. One and one-half planets to be precise. Or if all Earth's 7.7 billion people lived at the U.S. standards of living, we'd require four to five planets.[2]

Though the prevailing story has been gaining steam ever since it sprouted as a seedling in the rise of civilization about 10,000 B.C.E., it has never been the only story by which people shape life. There have always been those of our species who intended to live by following nature, not conquering her or even civilizing her. This story is the OneEarth story. Though secondary and often dismissed by MultiEarthers, the OneEarth story has proven to have great resistance, resilience, and capacities to evolve in each new era. OneEarth structures that support life by respect for the abundance of nature and her limits continue to be created. OneEarth is, in fact, a grand story

---

2 The Global Footprint Network at https://www.footprintnetwork.org/, accessed 7-29-2019.

that eclipses the grandiosity of the MultiEarth story against which we struggle for our survival.

The stories on the pages that follow embrace such a grand story and contribute to it. What follows are stories of transformation from the *bottom up*, unlike most, which are from the *top down*. The top does not want to be transformed. The current forms work fine for them. They maneuver merely to tweak what is, not to seek basic new forms of shared power in a new paradigm. The powers who benefit enormously from the way things are want everyone to believe that we all benefit too. So they repeat the story portraying the success of what we've been doing and urge us to keep doing it.

But the versions by Matthew and Luke do the opposite. They are clear that those at the bottom do not benefit from the way things are. What Matthew and Luke had to say appeared in writing around 75-85 C.E. Their Gospels grew out of groups and communities of people following the Way of Jesus. Jesus' life had impacted the people in these groups so profoundly that they no longer considered the Roman way to be *the* way of life. The Way of Jesus was. They knew they had been "called out," that is, called out of the empire and the idea of empires. Hence, the Greek work *ekklesia*, "called out," which we translate as "church." But when that word conjures in our minds the churches we know, beware. Many churches copy mainstream culture, imitate corporate structures, and justify racial and political discrimination. *Ekklesia* asks virtually the opposite of us.

The changes ran deep in the faith communities of Matthew and Luke. The followers became less possessive about money and ownership. Many became transparent about the wealth that they had acquired in the Roman economy and found ways to redistribute it through the community. Jews welcomed Gentiles and Gentiles trusted Jews. Slave were welcomed as equals. Women and men shared status and leadership. The tensions and wounds that had created so much separation when they lived by the norms of Roman society or by the rules of the Temple were transcended. As best they could, they put into practice the Christ consciousness with which Jesus lived. They understood themselves to be "in Christ." It was a different way of thinking and living and it transformed their actions and attitudes. The ego consciousness, as Swiss psychiatrist Carl Jung talked about it, was less in control. In Christ consciousness, they had the capacities to break through hierarchies of control and discrimination that held them when their egos dominated. In ego consciousness they could not break away from those authorities. Different skin colors and ethnic origins were embraced for the richness they brought to their communities. They had shifted out of Temple rituals though continued with many festivals and holy days of Judaism. They incorporated selected practices from their synagogue and also from the Greek mystery religions. They'd changed worldviews. They left the top down paradigm and became part of a new creation paradigm. In this paradigm, creation itself was rediscovered as the authority rather than the Torah or Temple, the Most High rather than any emperor in Rome—no matter whether they were called Augustus, no matter whether they were considered a deity, a Father, or a Son of God.

Only faint echos of these deep changes happen in Christmas celebrations across history, if they happen at all, so let's turn now to the stories of Matthew and Luke and examine more closely why their Gospels were so transforming.

CHAPTER TWO

The New Creation Via Women Who Subvert Male Rule

Imagine Writing the Birth Story 80 Years Later

Imagine being someone who wants to tell people about the birth of Jesus, but you are writing eight decades afterwards. You were not even alive at the time of the birth. So to plan your approach, you sort through the conversations you have had about it, and all the reliable sources you can find. That's the situation for both Matthew and Luke, the only two gospel authors to give us such a story. Mark's gospel was available to them, but he doesn't include a birth story.

You especially want to convey how different the world is for you and others who have heard Jesus calling them out of empire and into a new way of living. You are in solidarity together, having dared to leave much of the thinking in which you were reared. Now you are nonviolent dissenters from the politics of your government, headquartered in Rome and present in local governors, tax collectors, army legions, and mercenaries. It's made you strongly intentional about living in community with people and the Earth in a way that is mutually supporting. As a result, what you want to do is tell the story of Jesus' birth so that it will have the power to reshape people's ways of thinking and living. You want to show how it sharply contrasts with Rome's ways because they don't serve the outsiders, the dissenters, and the economic cast-offs. Yet Jesus did. You know how Rome depicts its glory, but you also know the empire's shadow side—a reality Jesus exposed in life and death. His breakthrough is at the heart of what you want to convey. If successful, you believe people will choose to restructure life by priorities apart from Rome's empire, different from imperial civilization, yet fully within the continuing regeneration of creation. As you see it, Jesus, living with an enlightened consciousness, did all of this. That's what drew you and so many to his light, which, in turn, lit your own. Now, how do you write about it?

So you rewind the story to when Jesus was born. You review the time Herod was King of the Jews, living in his palace in Jerusalem. He had built a magnificent Temple and it was the center of Jewish religion. Even though Herod was a terrible example of Jewish spirituality, he understood how to use religion to deflect resistance to him and even gain their support. So he built the Temple to assure that the leaders of religion would support him. Herod's sociopathic self was succeeded by his sons. Rome divided the realm between them. But when they proved less than satisfactory to Rome, it decided its own governors could better secure the empire. Pontius Pilate was the best known of these governors because of his role in the execution of Jesus.

These matters were on the mind of a Jew, who's been given the name Matthew (not one of the twelve disciples), when he decided to put into writing what he'd learned of Jesus. It was 85 C.E., or thereabouts. He wasn't interested in just sharing information. He wanted to tell the story loaded with the energies of transformation, because that's what he'd seen and experienced in his community of faith—where he and so many had come to think and live in transforming ways. Though they'd never met in person, Jesus had changed Matthew's way of living and thinking enormously, from the despair experienced under the thumb of Rome to empowerment in what can best be described as a new creation. And that was what and how he wanted to write about Jesus.

The 20 years prior to his Gospel had been exceedingly rough and chaotic in Judea. The Jews seethed with resentment toward Rome. Revolts erupted frequently, culminating in the first Jewish-Roman War in 66 C.E. and continuing to 73 C.E. After a Jewish rebellion in 66 C.E., Emperor Nero ordered his general, Vespasian, to lead his army against Judean pockets of rebellion opposing Rome and restore order by force. But chaos in the city of Rome also complicated things. Conspiracies developed that undermined Nero and finally caused him to take his life. A period of struggle followed to determine Nero's successor. Finally, Vespasian was declared emperor. He, in turn, put his son Titus in charge of the army.

With rebels in charge of Jerusalem, Titus laid siege to the city in 70 C.E., three days before Passover. The siege continued four months until the Roman army gained entrance to the city. Once inside, their first move was to destroy the Temple. The next week saw a ruthless slaughter of people, from rebels to frail citizens. Soon, the heart of Judea—their capital, Jerusalem, and their religious center, the Temple—was no more. By burning buildings, confiscating Temple and city treasures, and slaughtering people, the imperial army had destroyed the center of the collective Jewish identity. A way of religious ritual and worship, for many Jews, was gone. No more system of animal sacrifices. The Temple's attending priesthood was gone. A way of life had ended. Any who survived, fled the city. Only part of the western wall (today's Wailing Wall) and a few ghostly towers remained standing.

Imagine the disruption. The city's surviving residents fled and relocated. Yet again, Rome had shown its power through armed strength. An era had ended apocalyptically. Putting yourself behind Matthew's pen, everyone in the audience for whom and to whom you want to write still feels the cataclysm that destroyed their religious, social, economic, and political life. Like many of them, you have found it essential to be part of one of the many communities of faith in which followers of the Way gather. Here, the devastation was being turned into an opportunity for a new ordering of things. Here a vision for the future emerged. Here, the guiding story was not about an empire, but about creation and cosmos. Here, the spirit of the chaotic times was overwhelmed by the Spirit of God. In all these ways, the consciousness in these communities differed radically from Rome's Hellenic society.

Class distinctions disappeared. Slaves and slaveholders, former and current, served one another communion, the sacred meal. Gender roles were rearranged. To be sure, these radical practices were uneven and disputed. Even so, that they were happening at all burned into you the truth of a new consciousness. It was the Christ (Messiah) consciousness. Not only had Jesus compellingly lived this lifeway of equality, he insisted it was for all people and nations, not only Jews.

So how can truth so transforming be told against the backdrop of such devastation? What language can carry the illuminating, divine power of this story? That is your task if you are Matthew.

Matthew decided that like Mark, who'd already written his gospel, he too would send his story forth as good news in a time full of horrible news. As faith communities came to read Matthew's work, they affirmed the power of his presentation of Jesus by calling it "gospel." Mark had put together his version of Jesus stories 15 years before Matthew's. Up to that time, the primary use of the word "gospel" was by the Roman armies to report the "good news" of their military successes. Squelching the revolts of Jews by successfully laying siege to Jerusalem, destroying the Temple, confiscating its treasures, leaving the city ruined beyond recognition, and striking at the heart of Jewishness was, in the Roman army's way of thinking, a gospel story. Given this militaristic and political use of "gospel," Mark had been bold in purposely calling his counter story a gospel. There could be no mistake in the minds of Mark's audience that he wanted them to understand that the Way of Jesus was a more effective nonviolent alternative, not only to Rome's political, economic, and militaristic way, but also to violent revolts against it. Mark's successors, Matthew and Luke, both borrowed material from him and added to it. All three presented Jesus' way of thinking and being as a victory not only over Rome, but over armies and empires, over politics and economics everywhere at any time, including today's superpowers and growth economics. It was a powerful affirmation of Matthew's version when it, too, came to be called "gospel," even though he hadn't used the word himself.

Before moving on, I want to emphasize that imagining ourselves as one of these Gospel authors is not just an exercise in fantasy. It releases in us the imagination we need to live the Christ consciousness today, when a greater destruction than that of Jerusalem and the Temple is happening in creation. Our civilization has taxed creation far beyond what she can bear. If we can open our eyes to see what the gospel authors were doing as they told the story of the birth of Jesus, then we are much more likely to know how to tell the story today. We are more likely to live animated by the grand, evolutionary story of all of creation. Telling the transforming story and living it invigorates our souls for the challenges we face.

A Bold Opening to a Transforming Story

The experience of Jesus was for Matthew nothing less than a new beginning for the world, a new creation. Being part of a faith community made up of followers of Jesus' Way gave him personal experience in being part of a new humanity and living with a new consciousness that left empires behind. Matthew wanted to begin his gospel showing immediately that this new humanity was underway, despite the desolation of Judea. What better way than to create parallels with Genesis, the Jewish book of creation and the origins of humanity?

In the 6th century B.C.E., Genesis had done something similar to what Matthew intended. Then Jews of Jerusalem were taken captive by the empire of Babylon and forcibly exiled the many miles to Babylon. As happened with the 70 C.E. devastation by the Roman army, Babylon's destruction of Jerusalem six centuries earlier also struck at the soul of who they were. They'd believed that Jerusalem and their Temple were special in the heart of Yahweh, in essence, where Yahweh dwelled. So they reasoned that their city and Temple would always be secure. They believed themselves to be an exceptional people. But Babylon's invasion shattered that belief. Taken captive and forced into residence in Babylon, they heard their conquerors claim how Babylon ruled because the Babylonian gods had ordained it. They heard the Babylonia story of creation in which the gods warred violently until Marduk prevailed and defeated Tiamat, the dragon of chaos. From the remains of Tiamat, Marduk created the sky. Then, another god was sacrificed, and from that god's blood humans were made. Finally, Marduk ordered lesser gods to build Babylon, especially for him. This Babylonian story of creation, called the *Enuma Elish*, described creativity resulting from violent struggle.[3] It justified then what is

---

3   "Enuma Elis" in *Wikipedia* is a quick source to give a more complete account of the Babylonian creation story, the oldest creation story in writing. Accessed 6-6-2019.

still a contemporary belief for some that violence, horrible as it is, is redemptive.

But the Jews in Babylon couldn't agree with that. In protest, they put together their own story in which God called the world into being ("Let there be …") and delighted in all of it. No violence. No justification of kings or empires. But strong in the power of a loving creation, whose evolutionary processes bring forth a diversity of beings and do so with joy. The stories told in Genesis, which means *origins*, describe not only the cosmic origins of Earth, of great biodiversity, and of humans, but also the origins of many peoples, including the Jews. In addition, Genesis reveals not only one worldview focused on creation (OneEarth), but the origins of another worldview intent on building cities and empires, managing land for agricultural production, and using technologies and trade to gain advantage over others (MultiEarth) instead of fostering cooperation. Genesis explained not only the origins of humanity and, to the Jews, their origins as a people, but also the origin of an empire like Babylon which held them in bondage and subservience. It served them (and us) not only as a powerful collection of origins and identity, but also laid out the consequences of two worldviews, two lifeways, by which to orient life and societies. It continues today to show the importance of choosing the lifeway focused on and rooted in creation, instead of pursuing the way of empires.

That story of Genesis inspired Matthew. He wanted his gospel not only to protest Rome's imperial story, but also to solidify the origins of a new choice and a new way. He'd experienced the consciousness of Jesus in action. Not only did it counter Rome's story, it also countered the Jewish story that spoke proudly of the period of their monarchs—especially David and Solomon—as a golden age. Those monarchs were, for some Jews, the model that a coming Messiah would replicate and build on. But Jesus' story, like Genesis, was anchored in creation, not in monarchs and empires. There was to be no violence, but a new creation that, as Jesus said, was not someday in the future, but now— meaning, the *next* choice we make, the *next* step we take. That's how Jesus put it to an audience in his hometown of Nazareth at the start of his adult ministry of teaching and activism (see Luke 4:16-21).

The Unholy "Family Tree" of Jesus

As Matthew opened his new creation story, he began with words that echoed Genesis. His opening statement—"An account of the geneal- ogy of Jesus the Messiah"—parallel Genesis 5:1, "This is the list of the descendants of Adam." By presenting Jesus with the same formula that was used for Adam, we get a clue to his purposes. He wants us to see Joseph and Mary giving birth to a new prototype of humanity, one that surpassed God giving birth to Adam and Eve as the grand mythic beginning of humanity in male and female as one. Like the writers of Genesis, Matthew artfully used the literary tool of mythology to convey truth too great for any historical account alone. Matthew proceeded to use a mix of historical elements, along with truth and wisdom, that both surround historical events and transcend or undergird them. The histories of the time didn't mention the birth of Jesus. Matthew puts it in a context bigger than what history can contain.

The writers of Genesis knew that how genealogies and origin sto- ries are presented can galvanize a people into joining the dominant culture around them or living in a new way, whatever the cost. The multiple genealogies in Genesis (chapters 4, 5, 10, 11, 22, 25, 29-30, 35-36, and 46) provided a framework for the writers as they blended mythology and history to convey to the Jews in Babylon of how hu- manity evolved in close relationship with the Earth and all the beings of creation, but also how the opposite originated when many chose a worldview of domination and ownership over one of cooperation and sharing in Earth's commonwealth. Matthew shows us the same choices. The Roman empire and the Jewish Temple were dominators; Jesus jolted and loved people into embracing a lifeway called out of empire and into community with all beings.

This leads us to a noticeable difference between the genealogies of Genesis and the one in Matthew. Matthew includes four women. Doing so is most unusual in Jewish lineages of that time, but it emphatically fits with how Jesus repeatedly empowered women amid an oppressive patriarchy. At the time, women had no legal rights. Legally, they were possessions. Illustrating this terribly sad and unjust cultural norm is a line in the morning prayer many Jewish men prayed at the time: "I thank you, Lord, that you have not made me a Gentile, a slave, or a woman." Along with the ethno-centrism and classism of this prayer is its extreme patriarchy. All are key building stones in MultiEarth domination. Matthew boldly fractures these building stones by including women in the family tree of a new humanity.

Who the women are intensifies the fracturing. Not Sarah, Rebecca, Miriam, and Esther; but Tamar, Rahab, Ruth, and Bathsheba. Tamar and Rahab are Canaanites, Ruth was a Moabite, and Bathsheba was married to a Hittite! The inclusiveness in this genealogy powers through nationalistic and ethnic exclusiveness. It speaks bravely to the new consciousness with which Jesus lived and taught, and which Matthew was eager to highlight throughout his gospel, starting with the opening genealogy. That consciousness takes us beyond superpowers, patriarchy, immigrant-citizen animosities, and economic class. It is a consciousness that is as capable today as it was then of including what the boundaries of ethnicity hold separate. It is a consciousness that cannot be held or defined by nation-states, empires, or superpowers, by patriarchal hierarchies or by social or economic class. It is a consciousness as inclusive as the creation that brought forth the Earth, the stars, and the entire cosmos. No one religion or people has a corner on it. It is a sacred offer to all.

Once I'd come to see the importance of Matthew's genealogy—something I'd skipped over earlier in life as boring—I wanted to take a closer look at the biographies of the women Matthew includes. Why do they belong in the "unholy" family tree of Jesus? What a revelation! Each of these women, along with the men to whom they related, was involved in scandal. They broke cultural norms. They stretched morality to fit their actions, driven by the precarious situation in which they found themselves. The Greek word for such scandal is *skandalon*, often translated as "stumbling block." These women were stumbling blocks to patriarchy, to ethnic purity, to moral conventions.

But here's the irony. All four women, when they came to a scandalous moment, stepped on that stumbling stone and walked right on, into a new consciousness. Others were forced to take notice. It's not just about these four women. That still holds true. Matthew saw how personal choices in scandalous moments open up an opportunity beyond the people involved. These women are essential and exemplary to Matthew's purpose of presenting a story big enough to regenerate all of society and all of creation. The women power a new "Genesis."

Each of the women in Matthew's genealogy made personal choices that regenerated society. Their actions required new thinking and released the energy to make change. They contributed to the Second Genesis, as Matthew saw it, because they daringly opted for the ethic of creativity over the ethic of wooden obedience to custom, religious practices, and social morality. Their actions disobeyed conventions and laws that enforced injustices. They were compelled to break "righteous" rules—the ones they'd been taught—and go against the consensus of society. They did so in obedience to higher laws of life—laws that usher in a greater consciousness and new creation.

The following brief biographies tell the stories of these courageous women. Their stories are now also being lived on the global stage as Mother Earth refuses to obey the rules of dominating corporations, governments, or militaries. She is leading the scandal of disobedience. She insists on a new story of origins for all of her beings. It's urgent that we hear the vigor of her disobedience to domination and join her magnificent, proven powers to generate a new creation.

Tamar: Exposing Patriarchy's Abuses

Tamar's story in Genesis 38 oozes intrigue, family dysfunction, and trickery. It revolves around the levirate law, so named because of its derivation from the Latin *levir*, which means "brother-in-law." According to this law, if a woman's spouse died, the spouse's brother was required to marry his sister-in-law (Deuteronomy 25:5-10). When it operated well in patriarchal cultures, it was better than a modern life insurance policy. While today a husband can buy insurance on his life to assure the economic viability of his wife and family in case of his death, continuing relationships with in-laws and community are not assured. Social vulnerability increases. The levirate law provided both economic and social glue for a community. A brother who refused to follow the law opened himself to public shame for putting his own interests above the wellbeing of his relatives and the community as a whole. Furthermore, this economic and social law was given divine sanction, meaning that to disobey it was to disobey God, so when Judah and his sons disobeyed it, Tamar exposed them socially, economically, and spiritually.

Tamar was a Canaanite, a people who met with great distrust in Jewish history, so when Judah's oldest son, Er, married Tamar, they formed an inter-ethnic marriage that was a little edgy for the time. The Canaanites were among the earliest people of the Israel-Lebanon region, going back to the third millennium B.C.E. But intermarriage with them was denounced by Abraham, who did not want his son, Isaac, to marry one (Gen. 24:3); nor did Isaac want his son, Jacob, to do so (Gen. 28:1). Judah was one of the blessed sons of Jacob, and when the nation of Israel divided into two kingdoms in 922 B.C.E., following the death of Solomon, the southern part where Jerusalem and Bethlehem were located, bore his name. Clearly, Judah became highly regarded in Hebrew lore.

We enter Tamar's story at the moment of her widowhood. Er, her husband and Judah's oldest son, died. Er's brother, Onan, Judah's second son, was now to marry Tamar, his sister-in-law. But Onan did not want to marry Tamar because he did not want to bear a child that would be considered his older brother's. Sounds like he didn't much like his brother.

When his dad stepped in and told Onan to have sexual relations with Tamar, Onan acted with unabashed patriarchal ego and decided to circumvent his father and the levirate law by spilling his semen on the ground rather than having it enter Tamar. That stand-off in family relationships ended quickly because soon after Onan died.

Tamar then turned to Judah's third son, Shelah, asking, "Will he marry me?" Judah stepped in again, refusing to give Tamar his third son. Since giving birth was the main way for a woman to evolve into respected female personhood, Tamar languished childless, while the men in the family failed in their duties to her and the community, protected in their disobedience by the powers of patriarchy. But their abuse made Tamar desperate.

Here the scandal intensified. Tamar challenged Judah's delay by dressing as a prostitute. She went out and sat along the road that she knew Judah traveled. As he neared the spot where Tamar waited, he approached her. He did not recognize her because her face was covered. When he propositioned her, she consented to have sex, but only if he gave her a couple of personal items that he was wearing. With these in her possession, if he denied having had sex with his daughter-in-law, she would use the items as evidence against him. From their sexual union, twins were born, one of whom, Perez, was an ancestor to Jesus. But these are only the highlights of the story. It is a must read.

Tamar helped Matthew explode the usual ways of thinking. He did not want the strange circumstances in the marriage of Mary and Joseph to make them the first family in Jesus' story to be involved in scandal, so he showed how scandal happened frequently in Jesus' family tree. Tamar refused to overlook how she'd been wronged by the men in her distinguished but patriarchal family. She exposed their male egos for not demonstrating a form of economic caring required of them. Then, like now, when the powers that be do not keep the high laws of life and love, the people have a calling to do so. Tamar did. Though ethnically the outsider, she seduced her prestigious father-in-law, not just into sex, but into compliance with the moral, economic, and spiritual obligations of his own tradition. She challenged patriarchy through the power of her sexuality, when the law failed her. The law, as such, was useless to her, since it gave women no status. Men had the power and would decide whether or not to enforce society's laws, many of which assured their continued control whatever circumstances arose. Tamar used a more primal power—an erotic, feminine energy—to demonstrate Judah's vulnerabilities and entice him into behaving rightly. As Judah acknowledged, when he realized he had fathered a child by her, "She is more in the right than I."

More important than the sex scandal Tamar initiated was the unjust patriarchal power she exposed, even though patriarchy itself continued to be the norm. She refused to stumble over the failure of men to live up to their obligations. Through her daring, she grew into greater maturity and called Judah to a higher path than he was on. It is the same kind of expose'of patriarchal abuse that Jesus exemplified throughout his life, an important reason his message resonated with the oppressed. Don't many of us have to be seduced into a greater consciousness, clinging to privilege, instead of honoring the most vulnerable or trying to serve the common good?

Rahab: Befriending the Enemy

You needn't be a regular at synagogue or church to have heard of Rahab. She has made her way into cultural lore as a kind of archetype of the whore, the seductress, the escort, the "pretty woman." As a result, we may stammer a bit when we come to her in this "holy" story. Why did Matthew want her unholiness in the family tree of Jesus?

First of all, like Tamar, Rahab was a Canaanite, an outlier to Hebrew identity and culture of her time. Secondly, that she worked as a prostitute further fit Matthew's reasons for including her. She gives the story an extra dose of scandal. She makes us take the story in a different and messier direction. Rahab disobeyed patriotic expectations. In the eyes of Jericho politics, Rahab was a traitor. She cooperated with the enemy and threatened city-state security.

Yet, it was through Rahab's disobedience that she moved into a greater consciousness, and into the security available when we befriend those we fight as an "enemy." With her in the genealogy, the birth story swells to much more than Mary watching Jesus in the manger while Joseph stands by, and we all sing "Away in the Manger."

As the story is told in Joshua, chapter 2, Rahab, the officials of Jericho, and all the citizens of this impressive, walled city had lived anxiously ever since a large encampment of Hebrews had located just across the Jordan River from them. Parenthetically, it is critical to explain that this description of Jericho was written looking back through the vision of Israel's monarchy, two centuries or more later. The book of Joshua, which includes a "holy war" mentality, tells the story as a conquering monarch or imperial leader would tell it—exactly that fit the era of David and Solomon, the two who expanded Israel's authority over others by conquest. It is the kind of story told in a civilization-based worldview committed to conquest and domination—a view that competes throughout the Bible with the creation-based worldview committed to cooperation and interdependence. The archaeological record of this era shows that Jericho was not walled at the time; so the so-called "conquest" of Canaan is a story enhanced with the mythology of monarchy. The archaeological record fits better with the description of entering Canaan in the biblical book of Judges, a book more connected with a creation-based worldview. Starting around 1200 B.C.E., the cities in the lowlands of Palestine lost much of their influence just as the hill country's population greatly increased. The Hebrews of the Exodus were re-entering Canaan during that time, and that is the context in which Rahab befriended "the enemy."

Continuing with the version in the book of Joshua, named after the Hebrew commander, sent two spies to the city to gather some intelligence. But word got to the mayor of Jericho that a couple of suspicious-looking men were in the city. He put the police on their trail. Thinking much like today's FBI and CIA intelligence gatherers, who do not hesitate to work with mafia or prostitutes, they checked with Rahab. Her house rested partly on the wall around the city of Jericho making it a strategic structure for passage to or from the city. Spies would be able to go over the wall instead of through checkpoints at the gates. Think about how long the U.S. Border Patrol would put up with her house on the wall separating Mexico and the United States., unless, of course, it served their purposes. Rahab, the police were sure, would know a good deal about the comings and goings of male visitors in the city.

"Have you seen them?" they asked her. "Yes," she said. But then quickly added, "They have already left the city." Quickly, the police made tracks out of the city gates looking for the spies, while Rahab went up to her loft where she had hid them. There she made a deal. "I know that your God is the great God," she said, "so when you and your people take this city, please treat me and my family well."

Her lies and crimes of protecting the enemy were clearly aimed at assuring her own survival and that of the family she was responsible for. Though she may have been more shrewd than spiritual, her appreciation for the Hebrew God was a commitment to life in a shaky situation. For protecting two undocumented aliens in the name of Yahweh, this prostitute and traitor was acclaimed as one of the few female heroines in the great *Hebrew Hall of Fame,* as it's called. That roster is dominated by males. We can read it in the New Testament's Epistle of Hebrews, chapter 11.

Rahab perceived the vulnerability of the control the city-state, Jericho, exercised over the region. Being indigenous herself, with an ancestry rooted in the patterns of wilderness, she knew the ingenuity of the people of the wilderness encamped across the Jordan. She knew enough to risk trusting these people and their God over the city civilization she lived in.

She cast her lot with the Hebrews, rather than with the Jericho police and the city powers they were defending. More than a choice to save her life and her family, it was a choice for a different worldview, one expressing a different consciousness by which people of the low-land cities and rural people of the hill country could trust and befriend one another. Ruthless conquest was unnecessary. Rahab embodied the choice for a creation-based worldview over the civilization-based worldview of domination. As such, she comically moves to a greater consciousness in a story otherwise rampant with the mythology of imperial conquest.

Her courage was great enough that she did not blink when two men, spies for Jericho's enemies, asked her to protect them. With her wits and wiles, she fooled the mayor and police of Jericho. (See Joshua 2:1-24; 6:22-25 for her story.) Rahab did what Archbishop Desmond Tutu once suggested to the police of South Africa enforcing apartheid. He spoke to them directly and invited them to join the crowds who supported a new country, one without apartheid. Tutu urged the police to join the winning side of justice. Rahab functioned with this kind of broader and greater consciousness.

As Hebrew history unfolded, rabbis came to love Rahab and assured her fame in the Hebrew story. They taught that she was one of the four most beautiful women in the world, and that from her offspring came eight prophets, one of whom was Jeremiah. Though the rabbis likely added mythology to her story in order to speak boldly of her ironic significance in the competing worldviews that comprise Hebrew history, Rahab's choices attract such enhancement.

But is Rahab of Jericho the one named by Matthew in his genealogy or did he have a different Rahab in mind? This controversy preoccupies biblical scholars. But maybe it matters less than they think. Modeled on the genealogies of Genesis, Matthew was connecting the story of humans with the story of the cosmos. He was intent upon shifting our consciousness from civilization's ways to a new worldview. Inviting his readers to participate in that shift, he could not sit still for historical accuracy. He took history and let cosmology explode it. Matthew could only smile at any concern we might have for correctness in his genealogy. He would say, "You don't get what I'm doing."

In Matthew's gospel, history shares the podium with theology, mythology, and cosmology in order to convey a truth too big for historical thought alone. In this respect, Matthew and the rabbis are of similar minds. It's not a matter of winking at all the moral scandal and impropriety in Rahab's life but of having our eyes popped wide open to see that her greater consciousness allowed her to move beyond the category of "enemy" in her worldview. In this shiftiness, she had a vision beyond the consciousness of today's global leaders in business, government, and military. Her consciousness could overcome enemies, not by defeating them, but by befriending them. Such consciousness dwarfs the narrow, ego-consciousness exhibited by the controllers of civilization who depend on tear gas and worse as they control dissenters, putting them into prisons, detention centers, Guantanamo, or gulags. Converting to Rahab's worldview calls on our deeper and better capacities—those that express a humanity able to befriend enemies.

Ruth: Advocating for Immigrants

Though parents are not likely to name their newborn girl Tamar or Rahab, an appealing romance clings to the name *Ruth*. But Ruth is hardly the story of a woman living according to middle American values. Her story fills only four chapters, the little Old Testament book that bears her name. There we can read the story of a foreign woman who challenges norms and uses her erotic power to assure financial stability for her and her mother-in-law.

The backstory on Ruth is that she likely entered the Bethlehem area with her Jewish mother-in-law during the 5th century B.C.E., the era of rule by Ezra and Nehemiah, when Jerusalem and the Temple were being rebuilt. It was a hard time for foreigners, much like today for people in the United States without legal documents or here legally as Muslims. The rebuilding project was necessary because the empire of Babylon had destroyed Jerusalem and the temple in 587 B.C.E. About five decades later (539 B.C.E.), under Emperor Cyrus, Persia invaded and defeated Babylon, made many other conquests, including Judea. Cyrus freed the Jews who were still captive in Babylon, and cleared the way for them to return to their homeland. He was trying to solidify his support and also extend control over the Judea region. Ezra and Nehemiah were leaders in the rebuilding project.

But the joy of return was not shared by all because the plans to redevelop the region of Judea imposed an imperial model that Persia could bless. As was the ancient custom for taking control of a region and keeping a people in submission, the Babylonian army had carted away the educated and well-to-do of Judea. Now, as many of them returned, the redevelopment directed by the Persian Empire favored them, not the common people who had continued living in the region throughout the Babylonian era. Not surprisingly, the local people weren't at all excited about being displaced by the citified, ruling-class folks returning from Babylon. Some displacement was inevitable to the degree that Jews migrating back from Babylon to their homeland needed land to live on. But the imperial model of redevelopment gave insufficient attention to the locals who had worked hard to make a living in the area during the time when there were no centralized powers in Jerusalem or Temple. To them, rebuilding Jerusalem as the center of rule and enterprise, and the Temple as the center for religion led by the priesthood and sacrificial system, meant upsetting their lives, taking the land, and bring in a new subjugation.

In all this turmoil it became extremely important to be able to prove that you were a Jew. Only then were you entitled to land and benefits that went with this "Imperial Development Corporation." It was as important to be a Jew in that situation as it has been in the United States to prove that you're a U.S. citizen. How else could Ezra and Nehemiah sort out who qualified to be part of the redevelopment and who didn't? The inter-ethnic, inter-marriage, and inter-religious nature of the populace of Judea complicated things for their imperial model. That led them to make birth or genealogy the first criteria to establish one's Jewishness; loyalty to the Torah and Temple were the second. Nehemiah even tried to make Hebrew the official and only language to be spoken, much like U.S. efforts to make English the official language, requiring all immigrants to learn it immediately.

Into this environment of restrictions toward foreigners that Ruth entered the region from her homeland across the Jordan River in Moab. She was one of many scrambling to put a life together amid the efforts of Ezra-Nehemiah to re-establish Jewish dominance in the region through their imperial model. In contrast to the Ezra-Nehemiah worldview, Ruth's story expresses the universal vision described in the later chapters of the Hebrew prophet Isaiah, where the consciousness of ethnic and national identity is superseded by a conversion to a universal identity in which Yahweh is the God of all peoples, not just some.

But let's backtrack for a moment to how Ruth got to Judea. Some years earlier, when the economy in the Bethlehem region had spiraled down due to famine, the Jewish household of Elimelech and Naomi made the difficult decision to take their two sons and migrate to the region of Moab. There they reinvented their lives in a foreign land; their sons married the Moabite women, Orpah and Ruth. But the experience in Moab suddenly turned tragic when Elimelech and both of his sons died, leaving three widows, not only to grieve, but also without an economic base for their survival. The extremely marginal status of women at the time made it difficult for a widow to survive financially, even more so than today.

With the collapse of her life in Moab, Naomi decided that her best option was to return to her homeland. She would seek the support of her extended family in Bethlehem, in Judea. But Naomi had not counted on her Moabite daughters-in-law deciding that their future lay with her. They wanted to migrate to Judea as she had done to Moab.

However, Naomi pushed back. She argued they would do better in their homeland. Orpah was persuaded, but Ruth insisted on going with her. Her words have become famous. "Where you go, I will go. Where you lodge, I will lodge. Your people will be my people, and your God, my God." Though we hear these words in some weddings, Ruth was speaking to her mother-in-law, not her prospective spouse.

When they arrived in Bethlehem, Naomi told Ruth that they had a wealthy relative there named Boaz who owned a lot of land. Ruth replied that she would like to glean in those fields, even though gleaning had the lowest social status of all farm laborers. In this way, Ruth made good on her pledge to Naomi that the two of them were in this together. With the mood of restrictionism being promoted by Ezra, Nehemiah, and the returning settlers, extra hurdles lay before foreign immigrants like Ruth. She couldn't be picky.

Quickly, Ruth discovered which fields belonged to Boaz. She appreciated his hands-on approach to make sure his workers left extra grain for the gleaners—more than the gleaning laws required. (Those laws assured that aliens, widows, and orphans could sustain themselves [Leviticus 23:22, Deuteronomy 24:19-22].) But it was still hard work, slow and physically demanding. In addition, there was an attitude of superiority among the farmhands as they looked down on the low-class gleaners.

Boaz noticed Ruth and asked his workers about her. He had already heard of her devotion to Naomi, his relative. Pleased that she was in his fields, Boaz invited her to drink water from the workers' pitchers whenever she wanted. He instructed his workers to pull out even more barley and wheat from the sheaves and leave it behind. Like "strangers in the night exchanging glances," Ruth and Boaz became attracted to one another. A courtship between landowner and foreign gleaner was underway as he increased the gleaning favors he granted and instructed his workers to protect her from sexual harassment by other male servants and gleaners.

At this point the story gets really juicy. Naomi and Ruth conspired to give the levirate process some erotic energy. Happily, Boaz was a willing player. One night when there was a party on Boaz's grain-threshing floor, Naomi helped Ruth look her loveliest and sent her off to the party. Ruth waited for Boaz to eat and drink, getting his fill and becoming contented in mood. In fact, he'd had enough wine that he did not go to his house. He was so content that he went to sleep by a heap of grain on the threshing floor. Once he was asleep, Ruth, who hadn't let him out of her sight all evening, lifted the covers near his feet and curled up next to him. When he awoke during the night—surprised by a warm body at his feet—he was delighted to hear Ruth's voice and was just as delighted by her daring, seductive actions. That night their romance moved to a new level and Boaz wanted to marry her.

But there was a problem. Boaz knew of another relative of Naomi who was a closer relative than himself. Under the law, that relative, not Boaz, had first pick—and duty—to Elimelech's family. At the public hearing on the matter, the other relative showed up to exercise his right to Elimilech's property. Boaz explained to all present that this relative had first right to Elimilech's property, but that Ruth, the foreign widow from Moab, came along with the deal. At that point the man lost interest, saying that under those conditions his own inheritance would be damaged. That cleared the way for Boaz. He promptly announced publicly that he would then happily redeem the land of Elimelech's family and that Ruth, the foreign widow, would become his wife.

Ruth and Boaz had to overcome the strong prejudice Hebrews had toward Moabites—one born long ago when the Moabites were hostile to the Hebrews of the exodus, refusing them food and water. As a result, Moabites were to be excluded from "the assembly of Yahweh even to the 10th generation" (Deuteronomy 23:3). In the minds of restrictionist Hebrews, this bias was instituted by Yahweh. Despite this, Boaz and Ruth violated the sanction, transcended barriers of ethnic purity, risked clucking tongues, and created a new social consciousness in step with prophetic visions that included all people. They used the levirate conventions in support of their own passion and courage. Then as now, disobedience of a prevailing consciousness, even one claiming divine authority, becomes the scandal by which transformation to a more inclusive consciousness happens. In this shift of consciousness, old wounds are often healed.

For her consciousness-shifting courage, Ruth fits well in Matthew's genealogy of Genesis-like beginnings. Writing as one who was seeking to live the Christ consciousness, Matthew broke with the dominant culture's worldview in which genealogies were male-only and Jew-only. Having already experienced the radical inclusiveness of faith communities that followed the Way of Jesus, Matthew put an inclusive family tree of diverse people into his gospel. He demonstrated a consciousness that requires advocacy for and inclusiveness of immigrants.

A lesser consciousness—one that makes ethnic borders and national borders the ultimate line for who's in and who's out—doesn't fit with the Jesus whom Matthew was presenting in his Gospel.

In these ways, Ruth is more than a romantic story of a woman overcoming great odds, being a lover and the beloved, and living successfully in a new land. Hers is a tale of how we can move to a higher consciousness in which national borders cannot define the nature of being human, nor how countries are truly interdependent with all others, no matter their rhetoric and laws. Immigrants and their advocates everywhere have this consciousness and act on it; many leaders of business, finance, religions, and nations do not. Matthew's birth story of Jesus reveals a border-transcending consciousness.

Bathsheba: Unmasking Israel's Model of Empire from the Inside

In the genealogy leading up to the birth event, we are not surprised that Matthew includes Jesus' revered ancestor, King David. But then Matthew tips us off that something unusual is afoot when he includes the least flattering, most earthy and ego-deflating incidents in this Hebrew hero's life. He does so with just one word: Bathsheba. It's a clear clue that something in the Jewish understanding of this hero is about to change.

The story begins late one spring afternoon: King David sauntered restlessly up on the rooftop of his house. Across the way, he sees a woman bathing and was struck by her great beauty. David did not hesitate. He inquired about her and learned she was Bathsheba, married to Uriah, a Hittite soldier in his army. Hittites were one of the subgroups of Canaanites whom David brought under his rule. Since the army was out of town securing territory from Ammonites, David sent for her. Whatever we imagine that first meeting including, it definitely included intercourse before she returned to her house. Soon after, her simple message to David was, "I am pregnant." That was just the beginning of the scandal in the royal palace.

David moved quickly into cover-up mode. He told Joab, his field general, to send Uriah home from battle, thinking that Uriah would be more than ready to have intercourse with his wife while on leave and so mask David's paternity. But Uriah's solidarity with his army buddies and faithfulness to his Hebrew king were so strong that he felt duty bound to sleep at David's gate, not in his own bed. It forced the king to take the coverup to the next level. He threw a royal party the next night and made sure that Uriah got drunk. But even then, Uriah did not go home.

Forced by Uriah's sense of military duty, David moved to an even darker strategy. He ordered Uriah back to the army with secret, written orders which he was to hand-deliver to his general. Those orders were a military strategy designed to assure Uriah's own death in battle.

When General Joab received these new orders, he knew they were wrong militarily. He knew some of his men would lose their lives needlessly. But he obeyed his commander-in-chief. He ordered an attack on the Ammonites with Uriah in the lead forces. It was a fundamental betrayal of his men and a violation of military ethics. In the attack, many men did lose their lives.

Joab immediately sent a messenger to his king with a full report on the battle. It included the news that David awaited, and by which Joab feebly "absolved" himself in the eyes of his commander and king: "Uriah is dead."

Like the other women in Matthew's genealogy, Bathsheba's story drips with drama. Fueled by lies, sex, and power, it is too good not to read the full account for yourself (see II Sam. 11:1-12:35). That account includes a strong rebuke of David by a courageous man, Nathan, who, unlike Joab, was willing to speak truth to power.

Skipping parts of the story, David married Bathsheba after her period of grief. Their child was born, but died in infancy. Later, Solomon was born to their marriage, the son who succeeded his father as king, and developed a kind of governance that was praised by all those drawn to empires and the luxuries afforded dominators. But Solomon's political and economic leadership was disappointing to all wanting to see the Jews model a different way of governing and living—one that was in step with creation and their own anti-imperial history, exhibited in the exodus from Egypt. David and Solomon governed much like the Pharaohs from which their ancestors had been liberated. Solomon enslaved workers in the building of his luxuries, including his celebrated Temple. His economy was laced with subjugation of people and creation, as well as extreme class disparity. David and Solomon forgot the repeated mantra: Remember Egypt. They forgot what all superpowers forget, namely, that forces greater than empires delivered the Hebrews from Egypt. Justice and the mighty hand of Yahweh had prevailed. The same forces are at work today as creation and Creator deliver the Earth from the strategies of superpowers aimed at dominating her and all species.

Through it all, Bathsheba became the Queen Mother in Israel's empire. When David died and Solomon was enthroned, Bathsheba continued to have privileged access to the royal throne. Just as she had unmasked David's ways, whether willingly or not is hard to know, she did the same with Solomon.

One of David's sons by a woman other than Bathsheba was Adonijah. Being older than Solomon, he had wanted to ascend to the throne, but David preferred Solomon. That competition for the throne did not end when David died. Adonijah sought to increase his power through marriage. He asked Bathsheba to request Emperor Solomon to arrange a marriage for him with Abishag, David's last lover. When Bathsheba approached Solomon to make this request, he had a throne brought in beside him in recognition of Bathsheba's power and influence. But then when she made the request, Solomon immediately recognized Adonijah's ploy to increase his political influence by gaining the allegiance of that segment of population to which Abishag was connected. Adonijah's proposal for this geo-political marriage infuriated Solomon. It was not that he opposed such marriages, as his many wives show; he just opposed them when they threatened his power. Solomon immediately ordered Adonijah sought out and executed.

Once again, Bathsheba, the Queen Mother, had exposed the frailty of empires. In her relationship with David, and with Solomon, she showed that the Hebrew form of empire was not an exception to how other empires ruled. It wasn't that the Hebrews could do any better with their empire. It was, rather, that empire is not a model able to energize humanity in the ways of Yahweh.

By the time Matthew wrote his gospel, he and others knew how Jesus had explicitly rejected the model of imperial, superpower government. Not only did he challenge the powers of Rome which would finally execute him, he also rejected the once proud Hebrew empire that peaked under David and Bathsheba's son, Solomon. He knew that it could not be a model for governments in a worldview that lived aligned with the ways of creation. The star over Bethlehem is very different from the star of David.

Bathsheba was the woman in the family tree of Jesus who gave Matthew all the reason he needed to show why the way of empire was not the Way of Jesus. Matthew recognized how Bathsheba was a heroine for all voices in the Hebrew legacy who consistently dissented from their empire or that of any other. Because Bathsheba exposed empire from the inside, Matthew gladly included her in his genealogy.

Still, I wonder what was in Bathsheba's heart? Was she flattered when the king invited her to the palace? Did she go eagerly? Or, as a woman with no social, legal, or economic standing, did she feel coerced by his power, seeing no way out except to go along? Did her heart sometimes bleed from being captive to the vision of empire herself? Or did she relish the change from a soldier's wife to becoming Queen Mother? Bathsheba's story lends evidence to the view of Jesus that there was, and is, no real way to diminish the control of imperial values over us other than to live according to an entirely different worldview.

Matthew's Genealogy Shifts the Messiah Out of Empire into Creation

Including these particular women in the genealogy adds to the new story of origins that Matthew is eager to offer. A big part of this new story was the nature of the Messiah. The word itself means *anointed one*, but was understood by many to refer to a military deliverer, which was why Cyrus, the Persian Emperor who freed the Jews from Babylon, was called a messiah. Was the Messiah to be that kind of emperor, but in the lineage and model of David? Or was *Messiah* a kind of consciousness, a divine anointing as lived by Jesus who, coming from the lineage of David, took the Davidic promise for a kingdom that would be forever and transformed it. Given how ruthlessly Rome had handled Jewish revolts in Matthew's time, it's not surprising that people yearned for a messiah who would come from the lineage of David and re-establish the Davidic dominance forever. Many had clung to this promise Yahweh made to David (II Samuel 7) as their hope for a better world. But Jesus looked at that violent history and put the Davidic promise into a different worldview.

Let's take a look at the strong emphasis on David throughout Matthew's genealogy and note how it clues us in to that important change in how this critical promise to David is being remade. The genealogy is divided into three sets of fourteen generations. But why? The first set ends with David. The second set begins with David and ends with the Davidic line of kings terminated by the Babylonian empire. And the third set ends with Jesus, the Messiah, the son of David.

Jesus did nothing less than redirect the hallowed understanding, contemporary to his time, that a messiah would raise anew the succession of Davidic monarchs and have the power to rule. Early in the teaching period of Jesus' life, Matthew tells about the moment Jesus held up a lily of the field and declared that Solomon in all his glory was not arrayed like one of these flowering products of nature (Matthew 6:29). It was a strong rejection of monarchy, empire, and governance shaped by the ego-consciousness of civilization. Jesus made clear his intent that he would not be king in that way. He didn't believe it to be the way of Yahweh. Instead, he embodied a greater, divine consciousness—a messianic anointing—in which monarchies, empires, and superpowers are obsolete. The systems of governance in his consciousness mimic the flowers of the field and the subtle, elegant ways nature rules her interdependent community of all living things. *Messiah* was the name of this divine way of thinking, actually a way of being that smacked of Divine Presence and anointing everywhere incarnate in nature. Jesus showed that such consciousness had the capacity to embrace a way of governance that was as eternal as nature herself—much more enduring than thinking of the Davidic promise as a new succession of monarchs or superpowers. Matthew's genealogy moved the Messiah from the worldview of empire into the worldview of creation.

The scandals provoked by the women showed how stumbling blocks can be changed into the stepping stones necessary to walk into a new consciousness—one that David never had, but that his most remarkable descendent did. The erotic energy of women provides a primal strength for that huge shift from one worldview to another.

CHAPTER THREE

Guides in the New Creation: Dreams, Angels, and Stars

Mary, Joseph, and Jesus Open the Next Genesis

Matthew led up to the story of Mary with a select group of women in his genealogy. Before moving on, let's recap what the four women he selected accomplished and let it lead us into Mary's story. Each woman challenged and countered civilization's ways of sidelining her. Each acted with both subtlety and boldness from a consciousness shaped by the oppression of women. By so doing, she exposed as false the imperial civilization's claims to make life better for all. Tamar showed the underside of a society made of patriarchal structures. Rahab raised us to the greater consciousness of disarming enemies by finding common ground. Ruth exposed the smallness of "civilized" empires when they require bloodlines or race to decide who's in and who's out, instead of creation's way of rights for all. Bathsheba unmasked the notion that any superpower can be an exception to domination via ruthless, calculating, geopolitical ways of being and living. The cumulative impact of all their daring actions crescendoed into intimations of transformation. They helped Matthew prepare the way for the new creation that begins with the joining of Mary and Joseph in marriage and the birth of Jesus.

In whatever way Mary and Joseph came together, they were soon immersed in scandal. Matthew conveys the birth as a consciousness-altering event for the parents and for all around them. Many who have studied the birth stories of mythology have pointed out that Jesus' birth story includes mythic elements. One of those common elements is divine origins. Noting such similarities need not cast doubt on Matthew's account, as long as we affirm our understanding that Matthew's unwavering commitment to convey transforming truth does not proceed by historical facts alone. History alone, essential as it is, cannot supply the spiritual voltage required for the transformation of thought, soul, and society that Matthew had experienced in Jesus.

Matthew presents Jesus, and hence the new creation, as a divine surprise and a social scandal. Though his genealogy is remarkable for the inclusion of women, his birth story focuses on Joseph—initially on how Joseph struggled mightily with what right living looked like once Mary surprised him with the news of her pregnancy. Social rules dictated that Joseph should end his relationship with her, protecting himself and patriarchy, but at terrible expense to Mary and women everywhere. As I've already mentioned, if he broke with Mary, he would have made her economically vulnerable and marked her as unsuitable for marriage in the future. It was even possible she would be stoned. Such are the ways of "civilization." These ways included not only social norms of the cities and countryside, but also the social code of Torah, as interpreted by the Temple priesthood and rabbinical synagogues of the time. Joseph, committed to the Torah, could not conscientiously waver from that righteousness; so he began to plan how to leave the relationship, creating as little fuss as possible.

Then he had a dream. More on that below, but the result was that he did a 180-degree turn and the two married. Their child was born. Of course, many continued to think of Joseph and Mary's first child as illegitimate. But, by daring to come together in marriage, the two of them moved to a new consciousness and lived by new rules of righteousness (right relationships). Like the women in the family tree of Jesus, Mary and Joseph opted daringly for the ethic of creative transformation over the ethic of wooden obedience to custom and social morality. The disobedience that they chose challenged obedience to injustices imposed by allegedly "righteous" rules, by their teachers, and by the consensus "enforcement" of society. Their continuing relationship and marriage shifted the worldview from imperial civilization's divisive ways to creation's interdependent web of all life. Living with such consciousness they reconfigure what is possible, and stir the pot of the Jewish lifeway to embrace a lifeway open to any of us.

Significantly, Joseph's decision regarding Mary is our decision today regarding the Earth. When we realize we have no life without her, do we not recognize the Earth as our Great Mother? Civilization's ways, dominated by patriarchy, continue to disgrace her abusively. By treating her as a thing to be used rather than a being to be loved, "civilized" consciousness cannot marrying the Earth. Consequently, civilization is "stoning" her in a dramatic way—her land, waters, and atmosphere. Loving Earth, not just using her, is a centerpiece of the consciousness or paradigm of creation. The paradigm is infused by Spirit. Just as the Spirit actively conceived, gestated, and gave birth to heaven and earth through her presence in the cosmic womb (Genesis 1:2), so also Matthew presents the Spirit involved in the conception, gestation, and birth of Jesus in Mary's womb. In the chapter of the new Genesis written by Matthew, he artistically and imaginatively presented us with Jesus living the creation paradigm from birth to resurrection. Carrying forward Matthew's work, the chapter of the new Genesis that is ours to write today requires conversion to that same powerful and larger Christ-consciousness capable of ending empires and bringing into being a new heaven and a new earth. The holy family we need now is not just the family of Jesus or even the human family, but the family of all of life. Both Eve and Mary are progenitors in radical creation stories. The new creation needed today certainly cannot be achieved without the generative powers of women in full partnership with all beings.

Now, let's move on to how Joseph's world changed.

Joseph's Dreams—Dreams Bring Greater Consciousness and Responsibility

One night, while asleep, Joseph's thinking did a U-turn. It changed the rest of his life. What had that kind of power? A lucid dream! In the dream, an angel's voice said, "Do not be afraid"—a standard introduction of angels to humans in scripture and an immediate indication that the fear-inspired obedience to civilization's powers was about to be overcome by a more liberating way. It would require nothing less than Joseph's conversion to greater consciousness and obedience to that higher way. And that's what happened! The divine voice of the dream said that Joseph was to go ahead with his plans for marriage. Mary was to be his wife. The dream required of Joseph a sense of rightness opposed to Temple and Torah as then taught. His sense of rightness was rearranged.

As we know, dreams are not a primary source of knowledge and decision-making in the civilization story. Though the value of dreams has been rediscovered and appreciated by growing numbers of people, it continues to be common to leave them as movies of the night that don't make much sense for our lives. But in the creation worldview, dreams bring to our ego consciousness those energies of our deeper self and collective unconscious that are at work below the surface of our awareness. The smaller consciousness of ego proudly considers itself quite rational and empirical. But the much larger consciousness of all of ourselves revels in extra-rational knowledge—in signs, symbols, and images—in addition to the knowledge of perception and reason. Dreams are the language and the videos of that greater consciousness, speaking and making images to expand the consciousness of ego, usually against ego's will and in ways that stretch ego's orthodoxy.

It's obvious that Joseph thought differently about the importance of dreams than many today. Why he did is important for us to better understand how Matthew uses the power of dreams in his gospel. For Joseph, dreams were messages from God.

As Matthew's gospel would show, Joseph and Mary had entered into a creation-based worldview and *Messiah consciousness*. The Divine Presence spreads throughout this way of thinking and being. As such, it opens vistas for living that few schools of civilization evoke. Schools of civilization most commonly function in a worldview in which we see ourselves as outside and over nature. But in the Messiah consciousness and worldview we see ourselves as within nature and part of her. Nature welcomes us into creation's life-sustaining, interdependent community and living systems. In this consciousness, many dreams have great value because we recognize them as bearers of guidance for our life decisions, as was the case with Joseph.

As Matthew tells the story, Joseph made four major decisions for himself and his family based on dreams. To appreciate that Joseph lived with a different worldview and consciousness, we need only ask ourselves, "Would I rely on the dreams that my unconscious gives me for guidance in my decision to marry? Or trust one of my dreams if it warned me of imminent danger to my family and told me to move them to another country? Or trust a dream that told me when it was safe to move my family back? Or selected where to live?" Yet, Joseph does all of those in the first two chapters of Matthew's gospel. Four separate dreams brought to his conscious mind material from his unconscious. As Joseph understood it, dreams were connections with God and expressed a voice and language used by God. That gave his dream messages a divine authority that he did not doubt nor disobey. As a result, he could act decisively and courageously amid intimidating fears.

1. **Marriage**—In the first of these four dreams, Joseph decided to marry Mary because an angel in the dream told him not to be afraid to do so. That's exactly what he was: afraid. Afraid of breaking religious laws and society's norms and afraid of what would happen to Mary if he didn't. But before he could act in a patriarchal way, a dream with an angel intervened. When he awoke, he followed what the angel said and moved beyond the consciousness in which religious laws and social norms required strict allegiance.

2. **Family safety via immigration**—In the second dream, Joseph decided that he and Mary must take their son and immigrate to Egypt as fast as possible. Jesus was on Herod's death list. Egypt was not next door, but the dream told him Egypt would be a place of sanctuary from King Herod's paranoia. So off they went to Egypt.

3. **Timing their return from Egypt**—The third dream happened in Egypt. It conveyed the news to Joseph that Herod had died and that it was now safe for his family to once again live in Palestine. This sojourn in Egypt was especially important to Matthew because it is another connection of the "Second Genesis" of his gospel with the Genesis of the Torah.

The Torah features another Joseph who also experienced life changes through dreams. His understanding of dreams triggered the animosity of his brothers, who sent him off to Egypt on a trading caravan when it passed through the region where they were herding their livestock. In Egypt, Joseph interpreted a dream that had troubled Pharaoh before Joseph explained it. The Egyptian ruler was so impressed with Joseph's understanding that he elevated him to a position in his "cabinet," administering agriculture in anticipation of the famine predicted in the dreams that Joseph interpreted for him.

When the famine hit Canaan (modern Palestine) where Joseph's brothers lived, the brothers heard that Egypt had food, so they came to buy some. On a second visit by his brothers, Joseph opened the way for the family to move to Egypt. At the time, the move saved the family from their distress. But then, when a new Pharaoh came to power, friendliness to foreigners turned to hostility. The Hebrews were enslaved. It set the stage for the multi-layered experience of the exodus from Egypt led by Moses, an experience out of empire and into creation. For Matthew, the sojourn of Joseph, Mary, and Jesus was in key ways a reprise of the ancient story, and furthered his belief that Jesus was key to a whole new genesis.

4. **Settling in Nazareth**—Upon returning to Judea, fear seized Joseph again. He learned that Herod's son, Archelaus, had succeeded his father as King. Would his family be safe? The fourth dream told him that Galilee, beyond the reach of Archelaus, would be safe. So he settled his family in Nazareth where he and Mary had lived before. It became Jesus' hometown.

In an outer world controlled by imperial powers and Jewish tyrants who were hostile to him and his family, Joseph trusted his dreams to guide him to act wisely. He knew that his dreams came from a different psychic and spiritual space than the one where decisions were made by the emperor of Rome, the High Priest of the Temple, or the King of Judea. The space within him that gave him dreams was not bound by the fear that held people in subservience to the rules of the powers controlling imperial governments and Temple religion. It is essential for us to understand this space outside of rational and ego conscious-ness in order to be impacted by Matthew's story of the birth and life of Jesus. It is that same space that guides effective spiritual activism to-day and generates possibilities for shifting worldviews—shifting from ruling over Creation to moving within her embrace. Such relevance makes it a must for us to pay full attention to how Matthew mixes this vital element into his story—the genesis of a worldview that transcends the oppression of the worldview controlled by ego consciousness.

Let's leave Matthew for a moment to reflect on our world today. Dreams were nothing I paid much attention to in the first half of my life. I was introduced to their value by Morton Kelsey, an Episcopal priest, who had personally experienced the transformation of con-sciousness in his own life when he encountered the work of Swiss psychiatrist, Carl Gustav Jung.[4] Through Jung, Kelsey learned the

---

4   Picturing ourselves as a whole with two foci, Ego and Self, has been part of my un-
    derstanding since the 1970s when Morton Kelsey, Episcopal priest, introduced me to
    Swiss psychiatrist, Carl Jung (1875-1961). Jung's seminal contributions in the 20th
    century to the nature of consciousness, and how changing consciousness changes the
    world, continue to be advanced by many others. Jung and his spiritual kin have brought
    me ways of encountering and being encountered by the unconscious within me, as
    well the unconscious beyond me, called the collective unconscious. It acts collectively
    in the larger society to feed symbol-making and the "big dreams" that generate so-
    cial movements and moments, to name one effect. As I am able to take cues from this
    unconscious world, and integrate its messages into my conscious mind and heart, I

value of dreams. He came to understand that these messages from our unconscious are a way to listen to God today, not just in Bible stories. Divine influence is not, his writings emphasized, restricted to conscious, rational thought. It is the unconscious and non-rational where the symbols communicate wisdom beyond words.

In 1978, he wrote a small book entitled, *Dreams, a Way to Listen to God*. Because of it, along with another book, *Dreams, God's Forgotten Language*, by Jack Sanford, I was excited to learn of a whole other world to which I had access, but which I'd ignored. Sanford, like Kelsey, was an Episcopal priest who used Jung's work on the unconscious and dreams in seeking to reclaim the language of dreams as a source of divine guidance. Since then I've often received notice through a dream of a different direction I needed to go. A Jungian-oriented therapist has also helped me get the messages my dreams reveal. Being more inclined to rational intelligence myself, I find my default response is to repress the intelligence of the unconscious, gut, and heart. Dreams often intervene in my previous limited way of being and open me to what is far less comfortable, yet essential for healing and living more sensitively.

But in the MultiEarth world of Ego consciousness, it's common to laugh at our dreams and talk about them as curious, strange stories of the night—if we remember them at all. We call nightmares "bad dreams." We want to get away from them. But in the consciousness where dream messages are regarded as essential for living more wisely, nightmares are invaluable. They express information from our unconscious that we've long ignored. The energies behind that information are tired of being ignored and know that we are harming ourselves by

---

experience ongoing conversion in my relationships and actions. Matthew's attention to dreams is an important part of a story that takes life into a new spiritual topography and makes sense to me.

ignoring them. Finally, they act out into a vivid, frightening dream. Seen in this light, a nightmare becomes a treasure.

A major challenge for us with dreams is that they speak mostly in the language of symbols. The dream-maker of the unconscious is a wise playwright. The resulting videos and images that move across our unconscious mind every night are one of the most amazing phenomena of our lives. Words are infrequent. The symbols and images have layers of meaning. The context of our lives determines the meaning we are to take from the dream. Typically, our egos resist what the dream brings. Sometimes furiously so. Our egos do not like to see our lives stretched beyond what it can consciously control. But its control is no match for the unconscious. Unconscious energies persist in out-flanking, outwitting Ego's domination and rising into our lives unexpectedly. Often, information from our unconscious guides us in a trustworthy new way, even where it seems there is no way.

Valuable as ego consciousness is in giving us a sense of identity and ordering the details of our lives, it is our soul consciousness that is immeasurably larger, and has capabilities that dwarf ego. Soul consciousness offers us a sense of identity that enables us to feel we can live out of and up to that for which we have come into the world. We connect with the Divine call and purpose. We no longer think of spirituality as outside us or the world, but recognize that it infuses everything. Our souls connect with what is beyond us, as well as being part of what is deep within us. Soul-thinking can hold opposites in tension and in dialogue with one another. From that comes a resolution in which the opposites are part of a larger unity and whole. Our souls welcome what is beyond reason, what enters our lives from the unconscious, what transcends ego knowledge and thinking—all of which dreams do so well.

Getting back to Joseph, he shows excellent capacities to go beyond ego consciousness and recognize the revelatory capacity of his dreams. What a different outcome happened for Mary because of a different consciousness that could transcend ego's power. As a result, Joseph and Mary became transformers of society, raising Jesus and the rest of their offspring. Living in this larger topography of consciousness, Mary came, in time, to carry the feminine archetype in ways that continue to the present to be transformative across cultures. It's also true that a frightened patriarch and some imperialistic expressions of church have neutralized the archetypal power of Mary, idealizing her, which is, in fact, to neutralize her numinous power. But in the hearts and hands of those who recognize the topography of consciousness in which Mary lived her life, Mary brings power to women, a power that helps release them from the slavery of patriarchy and poverty.

Today, the decision Joseph made regarding Mary must be our decision regarding another mother, the Great Mother Earth. Ego consciousness is not able to be intimate with our Great Mother. Consequently, she is disgraced by the *Homo sapiens* to whom she gave birth. Our egoistic species is "stoning" her. Only by looking at the dark sides of growth economics and patriarchal oppression repressed in our unconscious can we increase our collective consciousness enough to move into deep love and union with Mother Earth.

Angels Bring Messages with the Authority of the Cosmos

Joseph's radical marriage dream included another element of transformation: The message was delivered by an angel. This is now the third transforming power that Matthew incorporates into the story he's weaving. He began with a selective, radical genealogy echoing Genesis and signaling that this story was nothing less than a story of new creation presenting a new birth for humanity. Then he added the vast energies and spirituality of the unconscious as he portrayed Joseph embracing the extra-rational revelations of dreams as messages from God. Now he introduces an angel, taking us into the world of cosmology, a world connecting the heavens and the Earth, emphasizing their unity.

The world of cosmology differs wildly from the world of history. Though lots of effort has gone into locating the birth of Jesus precisely in history, the gospel writers had a much different concern, namely, how to break their story out of the confines of history. That's why cosmology pervades the birth story. Think about it. History gets told by the dominant powers. So, like the leaders of today, the Roman and Jewish leaders told history. The gospel writers exploded it. They did not want the birth of Jesus to be confined to how the empire or Temple would tell the story. If we were dependent on the Roman Empire's account of the birth of Jesus, we wouldn't have one. Matthew and Luke released the story from captivity to empire and history by framing it cosmologically! Ingenious!

In the cosmological version, angels make surprise appearances and stunning announcements. They come out into the heavens as a magnificent chorus and loudly sing politically charged lyrics, gloriously laughing at Caesar—all empires, in fact. A star gets the attention of foreign magi and locates with near GPS precision what was to them a royal child in Judea. Don't even try to make all of this fit historically. If we do, we are undoing the very purpose of the authors who knew they had to tell what subverted and converted history. Why try to make angels, dreams, extreme human jubilation, and heavenly phenomena reasonable in everyday terms, when their wild, cosmic irrationality is exactly what bursts open human civilization's efforts to standardize and explain.

Madeleine L'Engle (1918-2007), American author, captured the sense of this wildness in her quadrant

> This is the irrational season
> When love blooms bright and wild
> Had Mary been filled with reason
> There'd been no room for the child.[5]

Empires and cosmos have different objectives. Caesars and presidents deal with nations and powers, finding definitions that establish borders and boundaries for each. But the birth of Jesus is part of a cosmos that is an expanding, limitless, unfathomable mystery well beyond what any superpower has yet defined or managed. Cosmology, a combination of science, mystery, and spirit, is unruly, and that's what makes it paradigm-altering. Empires don't handle that well.

How different, then, are the gospels' story of the birth of Jesus from a strictly historical narrative! While Matthew anchored the story in history, he added the conviction that a new creation is underway; he recognized the ahistorical realm of the unconscious and let it direct key moments in the advent of Jesus; and he described events featuring angels and a special star in ways that reveal how Earth and heaven are one in his worldview. Nothing written as history does these things. Authors Matthew and Luke showed their genius by presenting Joseph and Mary on the stage of cosmology, not just history.

We do well to model ourselves on them in addressing today's ecological catastrophes. By rooting ourselves in a different way of thinking, and by living our lives by the enormous story of the cosmos, we

---

5   L'Engle, Madeleine. *The Ordering of Love: The New & Collected Poems of Madeleine L'Engle* (Colorado Springs, Colorado: WaterBooks Press, 2008).

can stare down the empire's and the culture's frightening destruction of creation, and the continual intimidation of common people, including caretakers, dreamers, and defenders.

Matthew's worldview has a cosmology that makes rational thinkers wrinkle their foreheads as it goes beyond the limits of conscious knowing. For Joseph, the authority to act boldly and marry Mary was confirmed by the authority of the cosmos. Angels deliver messages from the heavens—the Greek word *angelos* means "messenger." The source of the message is cosmic and divine. There was, Joseph knew, no higher authority, so it commanded his obedience. It usurped and upended the authorities of Temple, Torah, or Rome.

If the story of the birth of Jesus had been told from the perspective of the governing class, the agents of change Matthew employs would not have been used. Nor would the story have been transformative, not then, and not across the centuries. So, however you or I might understand angels today, they are a highly effective way to bring messages from outside of what human egos can control. Egos separate heavens and Earth, unable to fathom the interplay and activity of the cosmos. Matthew's greater consciousness knows that the different realities of heaven and Earth are, in truth, *one* cosmic reality.

That the birth of Jesus happened historically during the reign of Caesar Augustus is less important to the story than are the appearances of angels, the bright lights, the unique star, and dreams that guide human decisions. Seven to ten decades later, when the writers of the gospels set about their task, they presented the birth in the theatre of the cosmos, where it had a grandeur and might that makes a proud empire's story pale.

Recovering this cosmological dimension is part of shifting to a paradigm of OneEarth living that fits within our planet's abundance. Stories of the cosmos in the first century certainly differ from the ones scientists such as Stephen Hawking, Carl Sagan, and Brian Swimme tell in the 21st century. The study of the heavens by the magi in Matthew's gospel give us very limited data of the cosmos compared to the telescope at the Palomar Observatory, the Hubble telescope, or the telescopes on orbiting spacecraft that can peer beyond Pluto. Only in the past hundred years have we been tantalized with the knowledge that our own galaxy is just one of a billion, maybe a trillion, galaxies— all in an expanding universe.

Even so, the improved scientific knowledge of 21st century cosmology continues to ask the ancient, enduring questions, albeit in new ways. We continue to wonder: What are the messages of the heavens for us? What is the meaning of the infinity of the cosmos juxtaposed with our own finitude? Is the cosmos ultimately benevolent or not? How safe is our existence? Does the cosmos love or distrust the evolutionary processes that have brought humans into Earth's constellation of relationships? Cosmologists inquire into the origin of everything and then create the best story to talk about it. The story is continually on the move as it incorporates updates from the best empirical observations of science. But cosmology also ventures into talking about what is not known scientifically. A strong trait of cosmology is interrelatedness, how everything is connected to everything else in a cosmic community.

Cosmology, then, is science and more than science. Matthew Fox (1940-), priest and theologian, speaks of cosmology as science, mysticism, and art. The science is the story of the origins of the universe. The mysticism is our psychic response to being in this evolving, immeasurable universe. The art is all the images that cosmology awakens in us and in society. In Fox's own words, "A cosmology needs all three elements to come alive: it is our joyful response (mysticism) to the awesome fact of our being in the universe (science) and our expression of that response by the art of our lives and citizenship (art).[6]

The unity and diversity of the cosmos are equally beyond what any of us can hold in a single consciousness. Yet mysticism assumes it as a starting point. Mysticism is able to accept incomprehensible diversity as One, though cultures and religions call it by many names. Mysticism's approach to the diversity and authority of the cosmos as One is singularly, wonderfully simple. The relevance and authority of the cosmos for our lives today has been helpfully described by Thomas Berry[7] when he noted that all the stories by which we live happen within the context of the cosmos. It holds and defines our stories. But the story of the cosmos has no larger context to define it.

No wonder that Matthew and the dominated peoples of his time respected cosmology so highly. Those reasons continue today as we see that Earth's cosmological powers will not be bossed by our species. We have been the beneficiaries of the primary intent of the Earth and cosmos to evolve and sustain life. Since civilization has unfolded as a project unable to control ecological devastation, a new creation, authorized by the cosmos, is the imminent opportunity and challenge of this decade. Matthew's vibrant cosmology of his time urges us to include cosmology in our own struggle for freedom from injustices— from corporations and governments cooperating to enforce rules for profit, even at the expense of life. We're empowered to do so when we live in the much greater topography of consciousness where cosmology is the integrating, synchronizing, ever-generating force.

---

6   Fox, Matthew. *The Coming of the Cosmic Christ* (New York: Harper Collins Publishers, 1988), 1.

7   Thomas Berry (1914-2009) was a cultural historian. Among his books, *Dream of the Earth* and *The Great Work: Our Way into the Future* have been especially influential on my thinking.

Earlier, when I showed how Matthew thought of the birth of Jesus as a second Genesis and a new creation, I did not explore the cosmology of the creation account in Genesis or the new creation vision of Matthew. In Genesis, the creation story presents, not history, but a grand cosmology—how all things began. The origins of humanity presented in Genesis are strongly antithetical to the Babylonian story of creation rising out of violence among the gods. In the Genesis cosmology we are created to be nonviolent, an image of God. That story still stands, even though the Jews and all humanity have certainly lost the profound sense that we are created with the capacities in our souls to be nonviolent. The history of human egos is painfully violent. But when we use the cosmological story as our story of origins, we can operate with a consciousness that transcends ego's narrow ways.

That's why Matthew saw the cosmological story of our origins reborn in the birth and life of Jesus. Today, the cosmological story makes us something far more than consumers or members of a race, political party, or religion. We can move on from such definitions given by our egos and the history shaped by them. Such transcendence is not fantasy. It has the deep authority of the cosmos supporting it. It breaks through the norms and authorities of today's oppressors, including the superpower systems tilted toward wealth accumulation, corrupt strongmen, and fascism. Cosmic authority is able to break nonviolently the tyrannical grip of prejudice, patriarchy, superpowers, bullies, and money.

Joseph and Mary continued to live their lives within the interdependence and relationships that are part of cosmology. They broke through the norms of society and showed there was a right, caring, and truthful way to live that reached beyond the norms that many had insisted were absolute. Joseph and Mary were criticized throughout their lives, and their beloved child would always be considered a bastard child by some. But in their consciousness, the cosmos' message of *fear not*, delivered by God's angel, won out over the consciousness of fear.

So Joseph's and Mary's encounters with angels connected them with the wishes and wisdom of the cosmos, even as it undermined the moral consciousness of the society of Nazareth regarding the norms of marriage. What was already conceived in the consciousness of the cosmos was connecting with her womb where conception was both a biological and spiritual mystery. They show us what it means to live in a *fear-not* consciousness.

Magi Act with the Authority of the Cosmos

Joseph was not the only one empowered by cosmic authority in Matthew's story. So were the magi. From some source Matthew learned about, he tells of magi—sometimes called "kings" or "wisemen"—in the East who saw a special star and understood its meaning to be about a new birth that would bring new leadership to Judea. It's doubtful that if the star was merely about a new succession of conventional monarchies that they would have been moved to make a trip of some length in order to "pay homage." Their desire to show respect in a public way tells us something of their hearts and consciousness. Through their cosmological understanding, this new birth transcended the usual thrones and nationalisms. The magi's wisdom recognized in the stars the birth of the consciousness they longed for. They felt deeply that they must stand with those in whom this new consciousness is happening and show their solidarity with this new worldview. It was to them a priceless treasure deserving worthy gifts of tribute.

The story has been a fascinating flash point between the science of astronomy and the studies of astrology. Not until the end of the 19th century—long after Matthew—did the scientific method separate astronomy from astrology. For most of human history, knowing the positions and movements of stars, sun, and planets guided human decisions in matters of navigation, calendars, crop planting, and life choices. When we apply the science of astronomy to the Star of Bethlehem, we swerve away from how Matthew was thinking and impose a method on the story that quickly misses its transformative purpose and power.

Nonetheless, over 200 books have been written on this star story and lots of observatories offer special December programs on the nighttime sky over Bethlehem. Former professor at Rutgers University, Michael Molnar, physicist and astronomer, made a special effort to think like the magi of the story when he programmed his computer to study the skies they saw. He tells about his study in his book, *The Star of Bethlehem: The Legacy of the Magi,* published by Rutgers University Press in 1999. The *New Scientist* website gave a brief description of Molnar's discoveries in an article by Michael Chown, December 21, 2001.

Michael Molnar, formerly of Rutgers University in New Jersey, is the originator of the idea that the star of Bethlehem was not a spectacular astronomical event such as a supernova or a comet but an obscure astrological one.

The event would nevertheless have been of great significance to ancient Roman astrologers. After studying the symbolism on Roman coins, he concluded that the "star" was in fact a double eclipse of Jupiter in a rare astrological conjunction that occurred in Aries on 20 March, 6 BC, and again on 17 April, 6 BC (*New Scientist* magazine, 23 December 1995).

Molnar believed that Roman astrologers would have interpreted such an event as signifying the birth of a divine king in Judea. But he lacked proof. Now he says he has found it, in the *Mathesis*, a book written by Maternus in AD 334. Maternus described an astrological event involving an eclipse of Jupiter by the Moon in Aries, and said that it signified the birth of a divine king.[8]

The double eclipse that Molnar discovered fits with the experience of the magi who saw the star and headed for Judea. Then, after consulting with Herod, the magi noticed that the star reappeared and led them to the home where Jesus was.

Regarding Maternus, Molnar describes him as a convert to Christianity who refrained from actually naming Jesus as the divine king he referred to, because his findings were astrological, something toward which many Christian theologians held negative views. Molnar's discoveries have been seen as a breakthrough in understanding the star of Bethlehem—it's timing, it's location in the heavens, and why the magi would have understood its significance in the way they did.

Owen Gingerich, a historian of astronomy at Harvard University, affirmed Molnar's work: "I take Molnar's work quite seriously. Anything he comes up with along these lines has to be considered as being very likely correct."[9]

---

8   This article is on the *New Scientist* website is https://www.newscientist.com/article/dn 1713-early-christians-hid-the-origins-of-the-bethlehem-star/, accessed 4/9/2019.

9   Ibid.

The success of Molnar's research can be attributed not only to his work as a scientist, but also to his willingness to take astrology as an important source of information and meaning in Matthew's time. Next, we go on to recognize how astrology was key to Matthew's use of cosmology in order to transcend the oppressions of King Herod.

King Herod Is No Match for the Ways of the Magi

The paradigm in which the magi thought and acted extended far beyond the imperial thinking of power and control. They thought cosmically, studying the heavens with the discipline of astrologers, and searching for meaning of events on Earth. Here again, Matthew shows that he is tuned in to a consciousness that thinks differently than the leaders in Rome and their surrogates across the empire.

As Matthew tells this drama, the magi came looking for one who was born to be king. Not being Jews themselves, and coming from beyond the geography of Judea, they did not bring with them the connotations of messiah that were rampant among Jews. But they came to honor the one "born king." Their understanding came, not from Jewish history, but from cosmology, their study of star movements and constellations. As Molnar discovered, the unusual star was Jupiter and it appeared in Aries, the constellation affiliated with Judea. The identification of a king in cosmology is clearly from a different paradigm than how the succession of kings and emperors happens in history.

In addition, Matthew is eager to show that the birth story includes wider geographies and ethnicities than Judea and Jews. The magi were from a geography beyond Judea, just like some of the women in his genealogy, and are another example of how Matthew decisively includes foreigners in his transforming story. Just where were the magi from? Molnar speaks of them as Roman astrologers, which may lend credence to the possibility that they came from Anatolia or modern Turkey. Anatolia is also the Greek word for "east." But the more common conclusion is that, since magi comprise the priestly class in Zoroastrianism, they came from Persia, home to that religion. Whether from Anatolia, Persia, or elsewhere, the magi knew well the rise and fall of kings and empires. They sought a greater consciousness in the heavens and practiced it as best they could.

In their journey of reverent solidarity across ethnic and religious separations, they miscalculated approaching Herod to ask directions. But why should they not have assumed that Herod, king of the Jews, would love to hear about a story greater than any empire—one with the potential to bring a new way of thinking to his people?

But Herod was threatened by the news. He consulted with his advisors who informed him and the visitors that Bethlehem is likely the place where the child was. Shrewd, calculating, and dark as ever, Herod asked the magi to stop by on their return from visiting the child and tell him what they found so he, too, might go to worship him.

With that, the magi were on their way. To their joy, the star Jupiter reappeared and they found the house where the child was. What happened must have been extraordinary for all involved, though no details are given. What Matthew does tell us is that when the visit ended, the magi had a dream. It is another moment in which the wisdom of the unconscious intervenes and changes the actions of the dreamer. The dream was clear that they must not keep their agreement with King Herod to stop by on their return and tell him about their experience. Knowing they must obey the greater consciousness of their dream rather than kings, they return directly to their own country.

Because of dream wisdom, they did not fall into Herod's trap, who is hopelessly mired in the empire's story. Matthew subtly mocks Rome's vassal, Herod, with this story. It immediately resonates with all who dislike this narcissistic sociopath and want to see him fail in his attempts to bring extreme injustices down on people.

How we tell the birth story goes a long way in determining its influence in our lives and institutions. When we tell the birth of Jesus as a cosmological story, humans are filled with awe and uplifted with the child, wondering about possibilities for a different kind of humanity and a different kind of earth. But when the powers of business and economics, along with socialized religion, tame the story from such wildness, humanity settles into being obedient citizens enjoying a holiday. Matthew saw the difference clearly. He refused any toning down of the story of the birth of Jesus. His burden as a writer was to present this as the radical good news it was in the middle of great breakdown of the Jewish systems and oppressions of empire.

We've had moments, have we not, when an experience opened our eyes to see the world so differently that nothing was quite the same? Matthew also, through the optical capacities of greater consciousness, saw how Jesus incarnated a consciousness that was free of imperial thinking and of many oppressive and exploitative Jewish traditions that had hardened into law. The consciousness Matthew urged his audience to shift to was called variously, "the Spirit coming upon me," "anointing," "Christos" in Greek and "Messiah" in Hebrew. Now think of this as a consciousness that doesn't just flash before you like lightening, but shines like the steady rays of sun and stars, not always quite felt or seen, but always shining and certain to be present again soon. That's the transformation of living in a larger consciousness, not centered in ego, but centered in our souls, where we connect with the cosmos and the Divine Presence.

CHAPTER FOUR

Angels: "Don't Be Afraid, You're Now Part of the New Creation"

Luke's Birth Story for "God Lovers": More Cosmology

More happened to Mary and Joseph during the pregnancy and birth of their firstborn than what Matthew tells us. At about the same time that Matthew offered his gospel, a person who's been given the name Luke wrote a gospel targeting a different audience. He begins by explicitly addressing "theophilus." Though "theophilus" could be a proper name for a particular person, it's more likely that it refers to people who were called "lovers of God," which is what "theophilus" means in Greek. Lovers of God refers to many people who were attracted to the life of Jesus, but who were not Jews. Nor did they intend to become Jews. Their lives were thoroughly intertwined with Hellenistic culture and Rome's imperial systems. For many, their livelihoods depended on participation in these systems. Yet, they declared their love for God, breaking in various ways with religious practices of the empire. Their ways of thinking and living had turned away from many of the allegiances typical for Roman citizens. They resisted worshiping the emperor or empire, and they were not drawn to Hellenistic mystery religions. They declared themselves to be God lovers. And, along with many Jews who had come to identify themselves as "followers of the Way," these God lovers also followed the Way of Jesus.

Such a choice had its risks. Throughout the first century, Jews and Romans held each other in suspicion. Riots broke out among Jews in Alexandria, Egypt, as well as in Galilee, north of Jerusalem. Rome's taxes often triggered resistance and uprisings. But no provocation was greater than when a Roman named Gessius Florus, procurator over Judea from 64-66 C.E., stole from the Temple treasury and murdered those who resisted this desecration. That led to a full scale Jewish rebellion in 66 C.E., which, in turn, led Nero to order his general, Vespasian, to lay siege to Jerusalem. The horrors described earlier as the political context for Matthew's Gospel were the same for Luke. Only the audience differed. For the people in that audience to identify with the Jewish followers of Jesus, also a Jew, was a choice of courageous proportions.

It was into this context that Luke sent his story of Jesus, especially to the God-lovers. The devastation of the Jewish culture and religion that had centered on Jerusalem had been a mere 15 years earlier. Passions could easily be rekindled, as the grief had not fully healed. Luke wished to present Jesus as carving a peaceable path through the tensions. He would show that Jesus selected from his own religious tradition the Way of peace and healing for all beings. Jews, Greeks, and all groups, whatever their differences, were one new humanity. It was what the Isaiah school of Hebrew prophets had imagined centuries earlier.

Gabriel Surprises Zechariah:
"Zechariah, Don't Be Afraid"

Luke's storyline introduces us to Zechariah and Elizabeth, and Luke joins Matthew in reframing gender. Their communities of faith were living into the consciousness of Christ in which hierarchies of male domination and female submission were being broken down. Paul, the Apostle, had noted this as much as 35 years earlier when he was writing a letter circulated among churches in Galatia (modern Turkey).

Matthew shows us this when he includes women in his opening genealogy and portrays Joseph as partnering with Mary once the angel has changed his consciousness. With similar thoughts of breaking through injustices based on gender, Luke opens with pairing a man's experience and a woman's. That pairing is an intentional practice Luke uses often in his writings.

Luke tells us that Zechariah and Elizabeth were both of priestly lineage. A special day came to Zechariah when his "clan of priests" chose him to enter the part of the Temple where the daily offering of incense was made. Because of the surplus of priests for Temple tasks, it was possible that a priest might be chosen to make this offering only once in a lifetime, so it was a big day for Zechariah.

But he didn't know how big. Zechariah and Elizabeth were faithful people, living ethically within the norms of Temple ritual and polity. But on this day, Zechariah had a cosmological experience. He was encountered by an angel. Transformational! His worldview didn't include angels really. But the angel at the right of the incense altar filled him with such fright and awe that it broke him right out of his Temple-shaped paradigm.

The first words from the angel were, "Don't be afraid, Zechariah." This simple phrase counters the paradigm of empires and temples that specialize in telling us that we need to do it their way or suffer the consequences. The citizens of empire and adherents of Temple worship live with a spirit of fear. "Don't fear" are words that defy the dominating powers who control us. Can we really look at those powers with a fearless spirit? Throughout Luke's telling of Jesus' birth, angels speak these revolutionary words, "Don't be afraid." Then they proceed to deliver a message from a different paradigm than the one in which their hearers are living.

So it was for Zechariah. The angel said that Elizabeth would conceive a special son. That he would be filled with the Divine Spirit while still developing in the womb.

Now Zechariah and Elizabeth had often prayed for a child. But Elizabeth had not conceived. They felt powerless to generate new life as they watched one another age beyond child-bearing years. So, in the face of the angel's jarring message, Zechariah understandably was flooded with doubt. He'd resigned himself to childlessness. But the angel said his child would live in the spirit of the great Elijah. He, a priest, wondered, "Would his son really be a prophet?" It was a challenging thought since priests frequently found prophets a challenge and too hard to control.

But at that point, the angel got firm with him. "I'm Gabriel," the angel said, claiming his full cosmic authority. Gabriel was clear with Zechariah that he was to move out of the past and live the rest of his life in a different paradigm, one of cosmic and Spirit consciousness. Temple "righteousness" was no longer to govern his life. At that point Zechariah became speechless.

Finished with the offering, Zechariah left the holy place by the altar of incense and went out to the people. They were familiar with how long this special time of daily prayer typically took, so they wondered what had taken him so long. They'd been waiting outside the sanctuary to be blessed by the priest-of-the-day, but when Zechariah finally came out, he couldn't speak. He couldn't give a blessing. When the people saw Zechariah in this not-so-priestly state, they concluded quite rightly that he'd had a vision, but they could only wonder what else might have happened.

After his stint of priestly duties at the Temple was complete, Zechariah returned to Elizabeth. She conceived despite their previous doubts that they were still within childbearing years. For both of them, the pregnancy was a mind-altering, soul-developing event. Zechariah remained speechless throughout her pregnancy, giving him plenty of time to contemplate and enter more fully into this new consciousness of the Spirit. Elizabeth, happy as could be, went into seclusion for five months, also contemplating life in a new paradigm. The paradigm in which she and Zechariah had been living had heaped disgrace upon her for being childless. But in the new paradigm, disgrace evaporated, and the generation of life began.

It's Gabriel Again: "Mary, Don't Be Afraid"

It was in Elizabeth's sixth month that Gabriel made another paradigm-shifting appearance. This one in the north country of Galilee, in the town of Nazareth, to Elizabeth's much younger cousin, Mary (Luke 2:28-38). "Greetings, favored one," he said. "What in the world does he mean?" Mary wondered. The angelic words followed, "Do not be afraid." Gabriel tells her that she'll get pregnant, have a son, and name him Jesus. Gabriel seems to be into naming babies. He told Zechariah that their son would be named John. Gabriel went on to tell Mary that Jesus would be great, called the *Son of the Most High*, and be given the throne of David—a throne that had not existed since the Babylonian Empire destroyed Jerusalem and the monarchy in

587 BCE. The kingdom of Jesus, according to Gabriel, would go on forever.

Imagine sitting still for that one! Gabriel is taking *kingdom* out of the paradigm of monarchies, empires, and temples—none of which last forever—and reframing it in the paradigm of cosmology and creation where "forever" can happen. This agrees with Matthew's genealogy regarding the shift in how "Messiah" is to be understood.

No surprise, then, that Mary was overcome and found this more than she could take in. Incredulous, Mary replied to Gabriel, "I've never known a man." But Gabriel was not deterred. He spoke with fervor about the great powers the cosmic paradigm brought to her and told Mary, "The Holy Spirit will come upon you. The power of the Most High will hover over you. Your son will be holy and called *Son of God*. And Elizabeth, your cousin, is six months pregnant even though she thought she was too old." While Elizabeth was old to have a child, Mary was quite young. But such perceptions matter little in the cosmological paradigm.

At every point the angelic message rebelled against imperial and Temple thinking and offered a better alternative. "Holy Spirit," "Most High," and "Son of God" were all politically charged phrases, and each one was far more powerful cosmologically than their political counterparts in the empire. The "Holy Spirit" generated life and liberated it, whereas the spirit of the age justified the violence of Rome's systems and military while draining life from the oppressed Jews and other conquered peoples. The "Most High" overruled the high priest, King Herod, and the Emperor Caesar who had just added Augustus ("Venerable and Exalted") to his name. And "Son of God" spoke truth to imperial power in that once the emperors were deified, their sons became "sons of god." Mary's son would be holy, or whole, in an un-whole society torn by division, racism, and isolation—all of which were internalized in how people thought and acted.

Clearly, these words came from a different paradigm than the one that had shaped Mary. Could this young woman shift her belief to trust this message? Yes, she could. What a transformation, one that would be repeated again and again throughout the ministry of Jesus in his adulthood, and continued as people like Luke heard the stories of Jesus.

A similar shift in worldviews can regenerate life on Earth today amid superpower destruction and religions that align themselves with the imperial paradigm and know too little of the cosmologically-shaped alternatives.

CHAPTER FIVE

New Creation Wildness: Mary's Economics and the Shepherds' Awe

Mary the Economist: Her Song Isn't Sung in the Malls

Gabriel's visits with Zechariah and Mary set in motion a series of events that involved one radicalizing moment after another. Luke interweaves all of them to boost the power of his story to tell what the fullness of life looks like. Gabriel gone, Mary immediately headed off to visit her older cousin, Elizabeth. Did she travel by herself? It was unheard of, but much in Luke's story is that way. When Mary walked in the door and greeted Elizabeth, Elizabeth felt her child leap in her womb. It was that same Holy Spirit that Gabriel had told Zechariah about. That Spirit animated Elizabeth to speak loudly, forcefully from the angelic paradigm: "You, Mary, are blessed among women. So is the child of your womb. Why does it even happen to me that I am being visited by the mother of my Lord? I say that, Mary, because as soon as I heard the sound of your voice, I felt my child leap for joy inside my womb! And blessed are you for believing what the Lord, through his angel, told you." What a greeting! In pregnancy and in this moment, Elizabeth was released from the consciousness that had kept her childless, restricted within the paradigm of empire and temple.

But so was Mary! Luke tells how Mary replied, exulting:
"My soul magnifies the Lord,
and my spirit rejoices in God my Savior,
for he has looked with favor on the lowliness of his servant.
Surely, from now on all generations will call me blessed;
for the Mighty One has done great things for me,
and holy is his name.
His mercy is for those who fear him
from generation to generation.
He has shown strength with his arm;
he has scattered the proud in the thoughts of their hearts.
He has brought down the powerful from their thrones,
and lifted up the lowly;
he has filled the hungry with good things,
and sent the rich away empty.
He has helped his servant Israel,
in remembrance of his mercy,
according to the promise he made to our ancestors,
to Abraham and to his descendants forever."

Three months later, Mary returned to her home.

The specialness of the poetic lyrics flowing from Mary in that moment has been recognized by many. Hundreds of musicians have put all or part of Mary's poem into their compositions, often calling them the "Magnificat," (in Latin) the first word from Mary's lips. An article in *Wikipedia* lists 233 composers and their compositions using these lyrics.[10] But economies, businesses, and governments have shown no such enthusiasm. What has inspired artists has left cold other powers that be, intent, as they are, on prioritizing ways to accumulate wealth

---

10 "List of Magnificat Composers," *Wikipedia,* accessed 9-15-2019.

and consolidate control at the expense of other more vulnerable people such as Mary and Joseph. The lyrics are nothing such egos can compose or emulate. Mary's words come from a soul connected to a sacred paradigm of equality, justice, and sharing—what we need urgently to be living today.

But was Mary an economist? Whoa Luke! What is this? Is Mary ever raised up for singing about overcoming class inequalities? Yet, she gives us the most direct economic message in the entire birth story. We cannot but apologize to her for ignoring that part of her exultation. We have ignored what gave her the greatest reason for her joy.

Mary sang in joy as she imagined her child advocating for a different distribution of God's abundance, a distribution through which all would have enough. This part of her song is not heard in the stories of Christmastime. Redistribution of wealth in any direction other than upward violates the commitment and economic model of the corporations running the world. But no corporation or empire has embraced Mary the economist.

If we embrace Mary's radical economic transformation, a deep conversion of mind and heart gets underway in us, moving us away from empire-think. In empire-think, wealth and poverty are accepted as an inevitable arrangement, even by those who despise it. Extreme maldistribution is so institutionalized in today's economic structures that any conception for change is repeatedly aborted before it is born. Yet, in the womb of Mary, the hope for change did get carried to term and resulted in a person living with a soul connected with the cosmos.

Her economic model assures that caring and sharing are able to shape a more just economy, and do so with the authority of creation and cosmos. And as Luke goes on to show in his Gospel, her son would teach and live such an economy, taking his cues from creation which the sabbath and jubilee economy of his scriptures also seek to embody. But congregations, whether from lack of understanding or intention, have selectively ignored the economy of scriptures.

The omission of economics from the spiritual life has devastating consequences for creation. Wendell Berry in his book, *Sex, Economy, Freedom and Community* (1992) pleads for correcting this omission.

> Probably the most urgent question for people who would adhere to the Bible is this: What sort of economy would be responsible to the holiness of life? ... I do not believe that organized Christianity now has any idea. I think its idea of a Christian economy is no more or less than the industrial economy—which is an economy firmly founded on the seven deadly sins and the breaking of all ten of the Ten Commandments. If Christianity is going to survive as more than a respecter and comforter of profitable iniquities, then Christians, regardless of their organizations, are going to have to interest themselves in an economy.... They are going to have to give workable answers to those who say we cannot live without this economy that is destroying us and our world, who see the murder of Creation as the only way of life.[11]

In this situation, described so clearly by Berry, we need to say together, "Let's welcome Mary, the economist." And some are doing just that.

There are, today, voices advocating for sharing, caring economies. There is abundant research on how these virtues are excellent shapers of a healthy economy despite the continuing reign of the military-industrial-growth economy. One such voice is Riane Eisler in her book, *The Real Wealth of Nations: Creating a Caring Economics*

---

11 Berry, Wendell. *Sex, Economy, Freedom and Community* (New York: Pantheon Books, 1992), 99-100.

(2007). Eisler shows how re-inventing economies to include caring and sharing makes good economic sense, as well as being right morally. Study after study confirms that such an economy is healthier for people, planet, and profits than an economy focused in competitive advantage and growth. The Swiss banking giant, Credit Suisse, provides an annual Global Wealth Report. It shows that the world has more than enough wealth to provide economic security for every person on Earth. Mary got it right. Her economics releases in us the deepest capacities we have as humans to live our best spiritual beliefs and inherent sense of justice. Her economics brings us into being truly human, a species able to participate in a robust new creation of Earth's creatures and processes of life.

So Elizabeth and Mary give us expressions of souls and consciousness where phenomena flourish that superpower consciousness doesn't much believe in. But believe or not, wherever the Holy Spirit and messengers connecting cosmos and Earth are at work, they dwarf the realities of superpowers and temples, despite any appearances to the contrary.

Think about it. What is there in these lyrics for superpower governments to like? Or for MultiEarth economies to relish? Or for businesses pursuing models of economic growth to rejoice about? Nothing. Only by converting out of ego consciousness do we connect with our soul's capacities to join Mary in her paradigm.

Notice, too, that Mary's lyrics are mostly in the past tense. From the perspective of the paradigm and consciousness of cosmology, the

- proud are already scattered,
- the powerful are already brought down from their positions,
- the lowly are already lifted up,
- the hungry are already filled, not just with food, but with good things,

- the rich have been sent away empty, and
- the marginalized and oppressed of Israel, who have not been co-opted by empire, have been helped according to the promise made to Abraham and his descendants (and here's that word again) forever.

Is the past tense wishful thinking? Or is it being prophetic about what will happen someday? Neither. Luke is resisting the imperial paradigm in which such questions arise. In the paradigm he so earnestly wants us to embrace, the truth of Mary's lyrics is underway in many of the ways the Earth and the cosmos function. Concretely, they are happening in the minds and actions of people living the OneEarth, creation-centered ways. The past tense shows emphatically the obsolescence of the reigning paradigm—an obsolescence we see around the world in the devastations visited on our environment by humans wedded to MultiEarth ways. What cannot be seen or imagined in the consciousness of ego and empire is apparent in the consciousness where the Holy Spirit, dreams, and angels' messages are welcomed as part of the mystery of reality. They are exactly the energies needed to move people into new ways of thinking and living. Luke put them into full service.

Mary Speaks to Weary Shoppers: Giving Is NOT the Meaning of Christmas

"We won't be able to have much of a Christmas this year" are words that come from the mouths of millions of saddened parents in December. But it's true only if Christmas equals buying and giving commercial gifts, or if the events in the stores and malls are the true Christmas event.

Corporations love a theology of Christmas that puts giving at the center. Whether the giving theology of Christmas emphasized the gifts the magi brought to the child, or Jesus as a gift to us from God, both serve all too well the commercial path of giving. The giving theology is exploited by thousands of ads, arousing the sense that we MUST buy something for EVERYONE on "our list." With 70 percent of the Gross Domestic Product (GDP) in the United States depending on consuming, the giving theme of Christmas has been exploited by an economy radically dependent on our buying.

Christmas is huge economic news. Depending on the business, 20 to 60 percent of annual sales come from Christmas gift-giving! Giving has come to mean shopping, buying gifts for family and many others. Though what we desire most cannot be shopped for, the economy of empire is in a full-court press every Christmas season to convince us that material symbols of our love and generosity are the essence of the season. We need to buy in order to participate fully in the ritual and spirit of the holidays. Ads barrage us with Christmas sales, Black Friday bargains, and marketing strategies of the empire's growth economics. All aim to get us inside the stores and walk out with bundles.

Economic indicators are followed closely every holiday season on the various business reports of media and magazines. Are consumers buying? Are we buying more than last year? Will merchants show strong earnings? Or do merchants need to entice shoppers into their stores with big discounts because economic times are hard? Indeed, weak demand from shoppers leading up to and during Christmas can result in stores, including some big chains, holding going-out-of-business sales.

Many people lament the stress of shopping. Though an element of good spirits and romance can be found in it, gift-giving can overwhelm. Each year people vow to do less of it. Some succeed. Congregations struggle to focus on the birth story, fighting the takeover by the shopping malls that make their rituals the primary religious rituals of the season. But many congregations fail truly to take back the Christmas drama from the MultiEarth worldview of the malls. Consider, for example, Christmas eve worship when the congregation is swollen because attending is a family tradition. The time, work, and money invested in such worship can be great, and worshippers may be polite and pleased to have been present, but going to church at Christmas is largely a part of the whole calendar of Christmas events—along with Santa, shopping for bargains, festive parties, lights, trees, wrapping gifts, and a wonderful variety of family traditions. The motivation to create good feelings and goodwill stirs in people's souls and ripples out widely.

Unlike Christmas, the birth of Jesus does not have giving at its core, but *redistribution*. Mary is strong on this. The economic injustices of class, so common-place in today's economic structures, are corrected in the story of a pregnant Mary and Joseph. Changing two-tier economic structures is very different from giving gifts and contributing to charities, unless those charities truly change the structures. The birth of Jesus is a story bigger than Caesar or the U.S. economy. It's a story of the birth of a Divine consciousness among humans that shows us a worldview in which we can live justly and abundantly, celebrate festively but not lavishly, and arrange our economy to care for all beings.

Christmas can urge giving to the "less fortunate," but the birth story urges changing the unjust economic structures that create the "less fortunate." Mary's economy redistributes Earth's generosity so all benefit from its fortune. The economic story, globally, continues to be one of growth economics. Whether it's called socialism, capitalism, or some other name, MultiEarth economics requires growth and pursues the falsehood that we can grow our way out of most every issue from poverty to ecological emergencies. The Christmas story has become part of this destructive paradigm.

But the birth of Jesus joins the Earth in speaking differently. The ever-expanding markets do not fit the confines of the planet, generous though Earth's resources be. It's now apparent that this expansion will be reined in by the Earth herself in this century. It is worth repeating here that the 2018 report of the UN's Intergovernmental Panel on Climate Change cited earlier in this book has given humanity a deadline. By 2030 climate change will have massively eroded Earth's livability unless we mobilize now and take dramatic measures to reverse climate change.

The birth of Jesus is a story of revolution that restarts the hearts and souls of people to align with creation, not Rome or Wall Street. Christmas does not seek revolution. It fosters feelings of goodwill within the MultiEarth world. Christmas squelches the economic revolution that happens in the Gospels of Matthew and Luke, beginning with the birth of Jesus. Even when churches urge restraint in consumerism, most are remarkably ineffective in releasing the transforming power of the song of Mary, where she proclaims that the poor are raised up and the rich are sent away empty (Luke 1:52-53). Current economies shun Mary's song. It's not possible to implement Mary's radical redistribution with MultiEarth thinking. Only OneEarth consciousness can implement the economy of the birth story and the essential changes to meet the 2030 deadline.

Toyohiko Kagawa gave his life to putting into practice such an economy. Educated in Christian missionary schools in Japan, he was drawn to the radical teachings of Jesus. Disowned by his extended family for his commitment to the Way of Jesus, he continued his education. After graduating from Princeton Theological Seminary in New Jersey, he returned to Japan and moved into a slum in the city of

Kobe. There he lived out the economic principles he believed Jesus taught. His changed consciousness led him into Christian pacifism, labor activism, and reforming social and economic structures. Among his books, *Brotherhood Economics* tells how an economic revolution akin to Mary's song can be accomplished.

> How can an economic revolution be accomplished? In brief, it must be accomplished by a change in human consciousness. That is, there must take place a fundamental revolution of ideas concerning wealth and professions in their relation to property rights, inheritance, and rights of contracts. Only as a revolution of these conceptions is organized into social consciousness, can economic revolution be completely realized.[12]

It is the birth story, not the Christmas story, that moves us into this kind of consciousness. It's the bold and wild spirit, not the spirit of the season, that can fuel an economic revolution for a new creation.

The Bold and Wild Spirit Empowers Marginalized Peoples

Step back for a moment and appreciate what's already happened in Luke's presentation. Gabriel told Zechariah that the Holy Spirit would be present in Elizabeth's womb, filling their son before he was even born. Likewise, Gabriel told Mary that the Holy Spirit would come upon her and be in her womb from conception on. When Mary greeted Elizabeth in her home, the Holy Spirit so filled Elizabeth that she spoke in a loud cry. Her words were more than her egoistic speech

---

12 Kagawa, Toyohiko. *Brotherhood Economics* (New York: Harper and Row, 1936), 78. Kagawa lived from (1888-1960).

or rational mind alone could know. Luke followed that immediately with Mary's song, which also expresses thoughts beyond what a human ego alone can deliver. And when Elizabeth and Zechariah told the circumcision party that their son would be named John, obeying what the angel Gabriel said, they had to do so over the objection of the relatives and neighbors gathered. At that point, Zechariah's silence of the past nine months ended. The Holy Spirit gave him words that flow poetically. He tells of the end of Roman suppression and coming into real peace, not the military version of peace-through-strength that empires impose. Zechariah also speaks to his newborn and tells him he will be a prophet. Given that Zechariah and Elizabeth both came from lines of priests, we can see that Zechariah was speaking from a new paradigm as he embraced the thought of their son being a prophet. He recognized that their son was to be a key in bringing forward the story of life for all people in a new paradigm where this was more than a promise. It could actually be realized. He spoke a profound blessing to his son.

"And you, child, will be called the prophet of the Most High;
for you will go before the Lord to prepare his ways,
to give knowledge of salvation to his people
by the forgiveness of their sins.
By the tender mercy of our God,
the dawn from on high will break upon us,
to give light to those who sit in darkness and in the shadow
of death,
to guide our feet into the way of peace."

Zechariah uses the same language as Gabriel, referring to "the Most High," affirming that their son would have a greater authority than the political and religious authority of the emperor or the high priest.

When Gabriel and Zechariah spoke of the "Most High," they spoke of one greater than Caesar Augustus.

As Zechariah continues, his words extend the "knowledge of salvation" not only to "his people," but to all "who sit in darkness and in the shadow of death." Many subjects of Rome felt they were in such darkness. The shadow of death was a steady presence in the lives of many. Turning from Rome's story to believing and living a story of liberation raised an unbelievable possibility: "Could this really happen?" What courage it takes to believe what has been previously unbelievable.

Luke adds story upon story of what happens when the power of the Holy Spirit overcomes the power of the imperial spirit. Zechariah, Elizabeth, Mary—and John and Jesus while still in the womb—experience that Holy Spirit. All of these events happen in only the first chapter of his writing. By the end of that chapter, Luke has left no doubt that he is presenting a story to counter Rome and the Temple with a way of greater consciousness and a different kind of peace than what Rome imposed. Like Matthew, his paradigm throbs with angel messengers from the Most High that break people out of the patterns established by Rome and the Temple.

Luke's wrap-up statement on Zechariah and Elizabeth is that their son grew strong in spirit as he grew up in the wilderness. It is not incidental that John grew up in the wilderness. Luke understands that the consciousness that raises up emperors and extends their power through military aggression, does not center on nature and wilderness. Temples don't center there either. Empires and temples concentrate power and money in cities. Throughout the history of civilization, as cities began forming after 12,000 B.C.E., cities have been ecological and economic sinks, whereas the countryside has been the ecological and economic source. Luke understands that for John to live into his anointing by the Spirit in the womb, he needed to be shaped by the rhythms and elements of creation, and by the friendship he developed with wildlife. His story has some kinship with the wilderness where Moses went after being raised in Pharaoh's imperial paradigm. It was there, after some years, that Yahweh came to Moses in a talking bush and called him to lead the Hebrew people out of the empire of Egypt. Once liberated, the people went immediately into the wilderness. Wilderness is where people get imperial thinking out of their minds and learn to live out of a creation-shaped paradigm.

Joseph's and Mary's Son Is Born

Luke introduced the story of John's birth by saying that it took place in the time of King Herod of Judea, who ruled by Roman appointment for four decades, 37 B.C.E. to 4 B.C.E., until his death. Luke wrote that Zechariah was a priest in the Temple system during Herod's reign. But when Luke introduces the story of Jesus' birth, he uses the larger context of the Roman Empire. That birth, he explained, happened in the time when Caesar Augustus was emperor of Rome, 27 B.C.E. to 14 C.E., when he died. Luke also connected the birth of Jesus to the time Quirinius was governor of Syria, significant in that it was outside of Judea and Galilee. Historians have noted confusion in these details because Quirinius became governor in 6 C.E., ten years after Herod was dead. Thousands of pages have been written about these dates. Some authors try to reconcile them; others show why that's impossible. But such a debate is extraneous to Luke and takes our eye off his purpose. For him, precise dates were less important than to show that the birth of Jesus was the antithesis of the systems that authorized Herod, Augustus, and Quirinius.

As Luke looked back over the 1st century from around 80 C.E., what he saw was sobering and horrifying. Though I've described the century before, it's instructive to read Richard Horsley, professor at the University of Massachusetts and an authority on the political, economic, and social dynamics of 1st century Palestine. He writes that Judeans and Galileans resisted Rome's imperial conquest, whereas other peoples gave in. The resistance intermittently flared up into revolts, which the Roman legions always met ruthlessly.

> In conquest and reconquest, the Roman armies systematically pursued 'scorched earth' and 'search and destroy' practices in order to terrorize the population and ferret out all pockets of resistance. The legions destroyed villages, slaughtered the inhabitants, or at least the elderly, and took tens of thousands of the younger and able-bodied to sell as slaves back in Rome and the rest of Italy.... Right around the time Jesus was born, in the area around Nazareth where he presumably grew up, the Romans had burned the houses and enslaved thousands of people in response to a widespread popular revolt in 4 B.C.E.[13]

This was the century that shaped Luke and his community. It was the century in which Joseph and Mary reared Jesus and in which he and John carried out their missions, anointed by the Holy Spirit to practice radical forms of ministry. It was the century during which Paul was born, grew up, and carried out his itinerant ministry among the many communities practicing the non-imperial paradigm, made especially exciting by the Holy Spirit's liberating ways. These communities

---

13 Richard Horsley, "The New World Order," in *The New Testament—Introducing the Way of Discipleship,* edited by Wes Howard-Brook and Sharon Ringe (Maryknoll, New York: Orbis Books, 2002), 1-2.

identified themselves as ones called out of the paradigm of empire and other traditions. Paul wrote his letters to them during this century and did so *before* Matthew and Luke presented their stories of Jesus. When Luke wrote, somewhere during the decade of 75-85 C.E., he was one of those called out ones. He knew well some of the communities of the Way that were dynamic, and therefore, continually bringing people into the paradigm of John and Jesus. The facts were important to Luke, but yielded to the elements of transformation when necessary to his purpose. It was the good news that had to come through. It was what was happening to people as they dared to move into the paradigm in which loving God and loving others as ourselves was the guiding practice. His writing was far more than the resistance to Rome that was practiced across the 1st century. Primarily, it was describing people liberated to live fully and to shape social and economic structures that worked for all.

Some Changes to the Story We Think We Know

The details, as Luke described them, differ significantly from the images of creche sets, the drama of posadas, and many other ways the "Christmas Story" is told. The story is often told in a way that has Joseph and Mary arriving in Bethlehem the day of the birth. Imaginations make much of the difficulty of the trip from Nazareth to Bethlehem for a pregnant couple. True enough, the trip took several days, but it should not be thought to have happened in the last few days of pregnancy. Most likely, Joseph and Mary arrived in Bethlehem a few weeks or even months before her delivery. Luke's phrase is simply "while they were there." Any thought that the birth happened the night they arrived can be laid aside as a misreading of Luke's words.

Another mistaken assumption is the notion of a stable. Much has been made of the dirty barn in which Jesus was born after being turned away by an innkeeper who lacked compassion for the pregnant couple. Luke, however, makes no mention of a stable or innkeeper. There's a good reason. It's doubtful either existed. Ken Bailey lived most of his life in the Middle East. For ten of those years he was on the faculty of Tantur Ecumenical Institute for Theological Research in Jerusalem. Whereas it is the tendency to understand Jesus and the New Testament through the lenses of our own culture, Bailey was ever insistent that we understand Jesus to be the Middle Easterner that he was.[14]

Accordingly, he did not picture Jesus being born in a barn, but in the home of a peasant family in Bethlehem. He'd been in such homes many times. He describes them as typically having one room, fair-sized, with the entry door at ground level and the living space a few steps up on a terrace. A loft or a side building would be for guests. Peasant families would likely have just a few animals—a donkey, a cow, and a couple of sheep. On cold nights or for security, the animals would be brought inside at night, remaining just inside the entrance on the ground level. In addition to the protection of their valued animals, the family appreciated the warmth the animals added to the house during chilly nights. Near the end of the living room where the animals stayed, a small cutout in the raised floor provided a manger or trough for animal food. The animals would be brought in as the last thing at night and taken back out the first thing in the morning.

---

14 Bailey, Kenneth, *Jesus through Middle Eastern Eyes: Cultural Studies in the Gospels* (Downers Grove, Illinois: Intervarsity Press, 2008). Bailey, 1930-2016, spent forty years teaching in Egypt, Lebanon, Israel, Palestine, and Cyprus. He also taught at Princeton University and several U.S. theological seminaries.

When Joseph and Mary arrived in Bethlehem, Joseph sought out relatives who quickly offered them hospitality. Anything else would have been a complete violation of peasant etiquette. Joseph was not really a stranger to Bethlehem after all. Luke claims he was in the lineage of David, who was also a Bethlehemite. In this vein, arriving in Bethlehem was a homecoming for Joseph. Families welcomed the couple as such. Peasant families of Bethlehem would never have allowed one of their native sons to go to a public inn, nor be put up in a barn—a building many peasant families did not even own. When the day came that Mary began labor, they were already appreciating the hospitality of one or more families in the town.

The word that is translated as "inn" in most versions, is the Greek word, *kataluma*. The word typically refers to the guest accommodations in a peasant home, not a Bethlehem motel. A different word, *pandocheío*, refers to a public accommodation such as an inn. It's the word Luke uses in the story of the Samaritan (Luke 10:25-37) where Jesus says the Samaritan rescued the man who'd been savaged and left for dead by the roadside. The Samaritan saw him, tended to him, and took him to an inn, *pandocheío*. As an aside, that story, too, fit Luke's purposes well because, though Samaritans were despised by Jews, here the despised one shows love to a Jew—something not currently pursued by border policies of the United States or many other countries.

Most depictions of the moment of birth in art convey a significantly inaccurate picture of what Luke and Matthew described. The scenes are iconic, and many convey a holy hush as Joseph and Mary focus on their newborn in a manger—often inside a stable. Halos often accompany the figures. Even if we understand them as representing auras, when halos are reserved for one family, that family is set apart from other families, which distorts the true nature of Jesus' family and all families generally.

Anytime parents are photographed holding their newborn in amazement as they quietly adore this new life in their lives, it is a sacred moment. Without taking anything away from the young family in Bethlehem, calling them THE holy family carries plenty of dangers. Wholeness and dysfunction happen in every family, as would have been true in theirs. The consciousness that makes only the family of Jesus, Mary, and Joseph holy contributes to damaging illusions and false ideals about "being a family." It reduces the shapes "family" can take—a serious problem because of the many configurations families, in fact, assume. Privileging this once-and-for-all heterosexual bond above all others inevitably persecutes the rest.

When Matthew and Luke wrote their Gospels, they were not creating an ideal of family, but one that was scandalously transformative. From Matthew's genealogy, we get the picture of a sacred, unholy family in which dysfunctions and irregularities become the path to a new consciousness for their lives and ours.

The moment of birth for Joseph and Mary came while in the home and hospitality of peasant friends. When the child was delivered, Mary wrapped him in bands of cloth, the common "blanket" for a newborn in peasant families. Then she laid him in one of the mangers carved out of the living room floor.

A Wild Cosmological Night for Shepherds

With the baby nestled in the manger, Luke shifts our attention to fields outside of Bethlehem where shepherds are tending their sheep. Events there affirm Luke's purpose to show powers that reach far beyond what an empire or temple can do. Luke set the stage. Emperor

Caesar Augustus exercised his authority over the realm by calling for a census. That brought Joseph and Mary to Bethlehem, the city of David, and in due time, the baby was delivered. Then the fields of the shepherds provide the stage for Luke to present the greater powers at work—those with far greater authority than Rome or Temple, able to bring great joy to all people.

The frequently heard description of shepherds as social outcasts may be overplayed. In various parts of the Bible, shepherds are spoken of with high regard. Jesus is the "good shepherd" (John 10). Even Yahweh was described as a shepherd in the well-known 23rd Psalm. Perhaps all the instances in the Bible of shepherds and their habits with sheep were used to protest the social hierarchy that considered shepherds of low regard. But more likely, some rules of the Temple in the time of Jesus made it impossible for people engaged in sheep herding to be considered "clean." Those rules are the issue. There's an irony in those rules, since sheep were necessary in some of the Temple's rituals of sacrifice.

Whatever their social status, Luke regards an angel appearing to the shepherds as just the kind of experience that makes the birth of Jesus completely radical and transforming. Try reading Luke's description out of a sense of hopelessness that was widespread in Judea, Galilee, and the wider empire. It seemed that real change was impossible. Liberation and a just life for all felt beyond their reach. But then there's a story that opens like this: "In that region there were shepherds living in the fields, keeping watch over their flock by night. Then an angel of the Lord stood before them, and the glory of the Lord shone around them, and they were terrified" (Luke 2:8-9).

Luke's description tells how the shepherds were shaken loose from the paradigm in which the underclass gets stuck where it is because real systemic change seems so impossible. But listen to the

words—"Angel of the Lord," "glory of the Lord," and "terrified"—
none of these describe the evening we'd expect were we to spend just
one night living in the fields with the shepherds. The role of the angel
is consistent: to bring a message of good news from another realm in
the cosmos. This angel, as were the angel appearances to Zechariah
and Mary, comes from Yahweh, the One who dwarfs the power of emperors and high priests and teachers of the law. This angel stands before them with the glorious presence of God shining all around them.
There's no fleeing. The presence stuns them, holds them terrified in
the moment. Nothing in their experience or imagination has prepared
them for this. They're shocked into openness to hear the angelic message. The stage of the cosmos has come down to their sheep pastures.
And the content of that message overflows with angelic authority:

> Do not be afraid; for see—I am bringing you good news of
> great joy for all the people: to you is born this day in the city
> of David a Savior, who is the Messiah, the Lord. This will
> be a sign for you: you will find a child wrapped in bands of
> cloth and lying in a manger.

Word after angelic word explodes in the hearts of the shepherds. As
was true with Gabriel's messages, this angel begins with "do not be
afraid." Of course, in that moment the shepherds had gone beyond
fear into terror. Fear was always a kind of invisible cloud of emotion
in the empire where Rome used it at will as the powerful and the military strutted their authority. It was also what the rules and laws of the
Temple produced: people fearful that they would be excluded if they
didn't live in compliance. So when the angel says, "Do not be afraid,"
the shepherds are immediately asked to do a 180-degree turnaround.

The angel's next word, "See," tells the shepherds that they needed to see with different eyes than the ones with which they typically viewed the world. He doesn't want them to miss the transformation of the moment, nor the promise of its impact. The angel's "see" is for all of us. Unless we see not only with our physical eyes, but also, and especially with our inner eye, we cannot understand the full picture. Luke knew that such seeing was essential to grasp The Way that Jesus would teach and live. Impossible as it seemed at the time, Jesus would show a Way to peaceful and strong defiance of Rome and the Temple.

Quickly, the angel's words move on to good news. We must not miss the political significance of calling a message *good news* or *gospel*, already described in the opening pages of this book. The gospel here is far greater than the announcement of a victory by the imperial army. It is an announcement of triumph over all things imperial for all time. If the shepherds had expected words of judgement when the angel told them to see, the good news quickly turned their hearts to joy—a joy not only for them, but "for all people." How mind-blowing for the shepherds to be the early recipients of a cosmological message intended for all people. In this universal message of great joy, no one group can lay claim to it for themselves. No less authority than the cosmos said so.

The shepherds, now spellbound, wondered what could this good news could possibly be. And then it came. It was the birth of a child in the city of David, or nearby Bethlehem. By affiliating this child with the leadership of David, the first thought for Jews was the hope that a successor to David was about to rise up and hold his own against regional adversaries—just as David had done. But that thought was replaced by Luke in the rest of his gospel. Jesus was not about thrones or armed battles. Instead, he would transcend the leadership model of David with a Divine consciousness of another Way—one as ancient and evolving as Creation herself. It would take some years, of course, before Jesus could explain how the universal message of the angels was about moving beyond thrones and violence. But teach it, he did.

Back in the fields near Bethlehem, the angel no sooner left the shepherds before an army of angels from the cosmos confirmed what the lone angel had said. Luke tells it like this:

> Suddenly there was with the angel a multitude of the
> heavenly host [or army], praising God and saying,
>
> "Glory to God in the highest heaven,
> and on earth peace, goodwill among all people!"

This wonderful song of glory to God and peace to the people is wildly cosmological. The vast chorus of cosmic artists and warriors singing "Glorias"—I mean, can we really imagine the volume of feelings pressed down into the lowest layers of the gut by a lifetime of imperial and religious intimidation would be released in those moments? What a moment of spiritual and political conversion to hear this great chorus sing glory to the God of the highest heavens instead of singing a national anthem or glory to nations, empires, or emperors! If we sing songs with the angel's lyrics, we need to ponder how nations continue to afford negotiations and diplomacy only a fraction of the money and energy given to the military-industrial-prison complex.

Luke's description of what the shepherds saw and heard deserves additional attention for how it exudes apocalyptic imagery and power, *apocalypse* meaning a stripping away of facades. The genre of apocalyptic writing, especially popular from the 5th century B.C.E. and into the early centuries C.E., was highly effective in resisting overwhelming force of empires, as it used imaginative symbolic dramas to describe greater powers than the violent imperial ones.

Throughout apocalyptic literature, a "heavenly host" has a military connotation in that the "host" is always able to defeat the war powers of evil empires that rise against it. The cosmology in apocalyptic writing loudly confirms that the powers of this world are not absolute, no matter how authoritarian their rule or how great their militaries and budgets. Apocalyptic writing, filled with cosmological action between heaven and earth, tells of the bigger story. That such actions in the cosmos are often not seen is more reason for the angel to tell the shepherds, *See!* Luke shows considerable mastery in keeping that bigger story front and center in his writings from beginning to end.

The army of the cosmos took on special importance for those with anti-imperial feelings by the time Luke wrote this story, given how the Roman army had razed the capital city of Jerusalem, murdered her inhabitants, and destroyed the massive structure of the Temple after pilfering its treasure. The hub of Jewish identity lay in shambles. What then could be more powerful than the armies of Rome? The people of Judea and Galilee had experienced firsthand what imperial peace through strength meant. Into the despair of this experience, Luke tells of the army of the cosmos singing over Judea a one sentence affirmation to the God in the highest heaven, not the one in Rome. Furthermore, the army of the cosmos could bring peace for all, instead of more violence.

One other part of the angel's message to the shepherds is essential to the story. The angel gives them a sign to help locate the child: "This will be a sign for you: You will find a child wrapped in bands of cloth and lying in a manger." These words tell the shepherds that the child is not in public accommodations, but in a peasant home. It narrows for them where to look. Sure enough, they found everything just as "it had been told them." Cosmology, not technology, made the connection. Mary and Joseph pondered it all in amazement. It was a night of awe—the awe that takes us to knowledge and wisdom that rational thinking can never know.

Simeon and Anna: The Bold, Wild Spirit Shows Up Again

The final episode Luke includes in his gospel regarding the birth and infancy of Jesus features an older man, Simeon, and an older woman, Anna. This is the second instance where Luke structured his version of the story to pair a man and a woman. The appearances of Gabriel to Zechariah and Mary were the first; many more follow. Because he wrote eight decades after the birth of Jesus, Luke had experienced in the gatherings of people who followed Jesus how women and men were bonding with a shared status. Because this was, and is, a radical departure from so much of the rest of society, he made sure to include this experience in story.

This second pairing happens as Joseph and Mary come to the Temple in Jerusalem carrying their babe in arms. They do so to follow the law of Moses regarding two rituals—purification for a woman following delivery of a child and redeeming their firstborn from the obligation that he be a priest. But Simeon and Anna intercept them as they enter the large outer area of the Temple.

Luke presents Simeon as a righteous and devout old man, words that describe a person faithful to the religious practices in the paradigm of the Temple. But he had a soul that also lived in the paradigm of the Holy Spirit. In the consciousness of the Spirit, it had been revealed to him that he would not die before he had seen Yahweh's Messiah. On this particular day, he'd gone to the Temple and when he saw Joseph and Mary bringing their son there to do what was "customary according to the law," he met them and took their baby in his arms. A prayer rose from his soul.

> Master, now you are dismissing your servant in peace,
> 　according to your word;
> for my eyes have seen your salvation,
> 　which you have prepared in the presence of all peoples,
> a light for revelation to the Gentiles
> 　and for glory to your people Israel.

Within the context of his time, this prayer from Simeon broke out of any narrow consciousness regarding the significance of this babe. He saw in this new life a whole new creation in which all are liberated from imperial ways. This liberation was underway, and it included all peoples.

Then Simeon turned to the parents with more unusual words: "This child is destined for the rising and falling of many in Israel, and to be a sign that will be opposed so that the inner thoughts of many will be revealed—and a sword will pierce your own soul too." All of this amazed the parents. In one episode after another, they could not escape that this birth was connected to other realms of consciousness and cosmology. What Simeon—a stranger to them—said about their child, and to them as parents, could only continue their journey into greater consciousness, both its joys and pain.

Next Anna, a woman of 83, began to speak to all around who were looking for a better way, what Luke calls "the redemption of Jerusalem." She was a prophet—a clear reminder that the voice of the prophet does not belong only to men. In this moment, she praised God about this child because those powers of redemption from oppression were being released into the world.

One of the reasons this episode was important to Luke's writing was the presence of the Holy Spirit in the life and utterances of Simeon and Anna. That Spirit would again be especially manifested, not only at many points in the activities of the adult Jesus, but also in Luke's writing of the "Acts of the Apostles" which presents a fascinating array of stories from followers of the Way of Jesus. Clearly, the Holy Spirit is a phenomenon of powerful opposition as well as an energy of new creation when juxtaposed to the spirit of the empire.

CHAPTER SIX
Reversing Ecological Catastrophe with a New Creation Story

How the Names Given to Jesus
Fit a New Creation Story

We do not know where the racing extinctions of species will end, but the ramifications and cumulative impact of their loss is altering biospheres faster than we can assess. Only in our blindness do we not see that our human species is included in that accelerating demise. In this light, the new Genesis, or the new creation story described by Matthew and Luke in the birth of Jesus speaks to our moment.

As I have demonstrated, Matthew and Luke show us how to move into this new creation story and its worldview, even as the industrial, technological economy and mindset work tirelessly to continue their conquest of creation and the displacement of species. Any time we narrow our vision to see history as the full story, Matthew and Luke remind us eloquently of cosmology and mythology. They show how the dreams of our unconscious are useful, even essential, when the powers that be impose forms of life shaped by ego-consciousness alone.

One aspect of the stories by Matthew and Luke that I have not yet unpacked has particular relevance to the new story we need in the 21st century. It is how Jesus was named and the meaning of several of the names referring to him in the birth stories. Let's look now at the names: Jesus, Immanuel, Savior, Christ, and Lord.

Jesus: Healing the Wound Responsible for Ecological Disasters

Naming a child is the pleasure of the parents, no? But neither couple with newborns, in the stories Matthew and Luke relate, does the naming. An angel preempts them. Zechariah and Elizabeth were told their son was to be named John. Mary and Joseph were told that their son was to be named Jesus. For Matthew and Luke, the naming by an angel is far more than a quaint detail. It is another element connecting these families and their sons with a realm of authority beyond empires. Emperor Caesar was given the elevated name Augustus by the Roman Senate. That came after his father, whose reign ended by assassination, was deified, which meant that Augustus was also a son of god. Other emperors also took to themselves, or were given, some sort of affiliation with deities. But none of these names for emperors carry the authority of the cosmos. The names John and Jesus were authorized by the powers of the cosmos and bestowed by an angel, a cosmological messenger. In the political context of 1st century Rome, it was of special significance for Matthew and Luke that Jesus was named by an angel.

Beyond the name itself, Joseph is given a reason for the name Jesus: "for he will save his people from their sins" (Matthew 1:21). Let's take a moment with the words "save" and "sins." These words have been so misused and diluted over the centuries that we need to erase from our minds whatever meaning they may have had for us. Across "Christianity," salvation has been more connected with eternal life than this life. And sins are far more associated with moral lapses than with the actions with which empires and MultiEarth living are shaped. Only with a fresh approach can we understand the radical significance of the angel's explanation for the name Jesus.

What happened to salvation and sin is another example of how the paradigm of empire and MultiEarth thinking takes over a story and guts the transforming energies by redefining, or co-opting, key words. In the paradigm of creation and OneEarth thinking, within which Matthew and Luke functioned, these words were on fire. The *sins* were all the ways, both personal and systemic, the Empire pushed people down, shoved them aside, and left them to struggle for life. And all too often, the Torah was an instrument of shame instead of empowerment. It was used to show people their inadequacies, rather than open doors to life. Jesus showed the Way to be saved from these sins and did it without violent revolution. He forcefully stood in the truth of unity with the Father in heaven as he refused to cooperate with the Father in Rome.

Today *salvation* must address saving life and livability on this planet as we face the existential fears and challenges of the potential death of a sustainable life on it. The Jesus story does this well if we enlarge salvation to address the death-wielding systems of MultEarth lifeways instead of restricting it to personal errors. *The same powers that put Jesus on the cross are the powers that are crucifying all species*—from polar bears to microbes, from butterflies to humans. Death by environmental destruction, pesticide poisons, and CO_2 excess could fill more crosses than the landscape can bear. Because his death came at the hands of these same powers, and his teachings took people on a path of life rooted in creation's ways of life, the angel's explanation of the name *Jesus* has a lot of voltage for this moment. *He will save us from the sins of MultiEarth living—those imposed on us and those in which we are complicit, or, for one reason or another, have not resisted.*

There is another layer of meaning in the words "save" and "sin" that has transforming importance for today. In Greek, the word *sowdzo* means *healing*, as well as saving. And "sin," *hamartia* in Greek, speaks of *getting off track, missing our purpose.* Think of the archer who takes careful aim but misses the targeted spot because he thinks it's something else, somewhere else. That's what happens if we shun the OneEarth call to come out of MultiEarth living. We get off track and turn away from the work that our species is given to do in nature's interdependent community of life. Instead, *our ego gets seduced into thinking it can improve on nature.* It's an ill-fated choice, separating us from creation. The damage of this separation is nearly as unimaginable as it is biocidal and suicidal. Its consequences are destroying life everywhere on the planet. We need healing. There's no time to waste.

Through MultiEarth ways, we have lost our saving relationship with the Earth, with the land, with all that makes breath and heartbeats possible. This separation is a really deep, enduring wound that's dropped out of our awareness. It lives on in our unconscious but is outwardly manifest in the radical individualism, painful isolation, and extreme disconnection wrecking people's lives, nations, and landscapes. Our wound cries out, consciously or not, for healing, a healing that can happen when we seek intimate interdependence with all that lives. For such we are made. Such healing is pursued in many venues, and the gospels of Matthew and Luke have a special contribution to make in that they explicitly lead us in peaceful revolution to heal the wound, calling us out of MultiEarth into OneEarth living.

We must understand that MultiEarth civilization is a torturous project, born of wound, and continues to wound all who participate. Ten to twelve thousand years ago, civilization broke away from creation. Instead of living interdependently with the rhythms of creation—her systems, plants, and creatures—some humans began what would be a millennia-long project of wanting to civilize and tame creation's ways. To their thinking, creation was too unpredictable. They began, therefore, to shape the landscape through agriculture and by building cities. They used new, emerging technologies previously unknown. Western civilization traces history back to that time. Everything before it is termed "prehistoric." We are taught that those actions in 8,000-10,000 B.C.E. were the beginning of progress—a trajectory of upward advancement that would continue through the millennia, culminating in the Industrial and Information revolutions and our high tech age today.

But what is missing in that summary is the wound. It dates from the time the Civilization Project began. I call it a "project" because it was not inevitable, but rather, a plan of *some*, not *all* humans. Others continued to live in creation-centered ways. But the "project" sought to improve on nature, or just exploit her regardless of benefits. It extracted excessively from nature rather than tending her in gratitude for all she provides. It set up its own rhythms and seasons, instead of studying the deep wisdom in creation's ways. Gradually, the project became the dominating power in human history. Humans have continued to develop this plan, shifting incrementally into more and more MultiEarth models and components.

But the kind of progress defined by improving on nature severed humans from the soil—described in the 1990 United States Department of Agriculture *Yearbook of Agriculture* as "a living geomembrane," which buzzes with processes essential to life. This geomembrane delivers nutrients to plants; plants, in turn, deliver nutrients to the animals, including us; the animals provide other nutrients to other animals, again, including us, in waters, which connect us all and on which every form of life depends; and land, that is, all landscapes, the peoples and species living in them, and all ecosystems. The severing from this geomembrane continues today as a wound so much at the core of human behavior that it is aptly described as original sin. Once we get submerged into MultiEarth thinking and living, that severed dysfunctional reality is always inertly there. We forget that we are made from humus (soil, earth); we forget that we have life because of the Divine Breeze and breath. We forget the combination of biology and mythology that describes the essential intimacy we have with the Earth. It is the civilizing enterprises that have continually pursued "improving" on that connection, but the result has been radical disconnection. We live largely unaware of how this disconnection affects us and all we do. The tearing away is so primal, so basic, that it can't help but be part of our separation from other humans, from all other species, and from Mother Earth herself. The torn reality shows up daily in the millions of actions and thoughts trashing creation. For this reason, Wes Jackson of the Land Institute in Salina, Kansas, says that "we cannot save our souls if we do not save our soils."

But so far, the adherents to MultiEarth domination continue in what is nothing less than blind arrogance of its ecocidal ways, insisting the damage to Earth, to all species, and to all humans is not the threat to life that it is. So thoroughly disconnected is their worldview from creation's laws that they believe they can lawlessly flaunt them. They've disconnected from the morality and love that would prevent them from shredding the bounty and beauty continuously created by the Divine and embodied in all of creation. The ecological disasters and emergencies of today all proceed from this wound and woundedness.

We're also separated from one another. It shows up along lines of race, religion, money, worldviews and more. Those lines aren't accidental, but dramatically and tragically intentional, designed through egos acting in fear. Wendell Berry, Kentucky farmer, poet, essayist, and philosopher, recognized the severity of this soul gash in his book, *The Hidden Wound*, 1970. He explicitly connected racism to the wound and how, humans suffering from this ongoing wound, though unaware of it, shape society.

The white man, preoccupied with the abstractions of the economic exploitation and ownership of the land, necessarily has lived on the country as a destructive force, an ecological catastrophe, because he assigned the hand labor, and in that the possibility of intimate knowledge of the land, to a people he considered racially inferior; in thus debasing labor, he destroyed the possibility of meaningful contact with the earth. He was ... blinded by his presuppositions and prejudices. Because he did not know the land, it was inevitable that he would squander its natural bounty, deplete its richness, corrupt and pollute it, or destroy it altogether. The history of the white man's use of the earth in America is a scandal.[15]

When we have been torn away from Mother Earth's nurturing by MultiEarth civilization, the steps are few getting to where we can tear up lives. Native American children were torn from their parents and put in boarding schools; there they were torn from their culture and identity. At the U.S.-Mexican border children are torn from the arms of their parents to be held in dismal, scandalous, genocidal detention. We are so entangled in the MultiEarth paradigm that we are anesthetized, even as we are torn further and further from our Source. "Progress" is rapidly destroying the very life that civilization claims

---

15 Berry, Wendell. *The Hidden Wound* (New York: North Point Press, 1970), 105.

it is improving. The Earth is in massive revolt against such civilizing. Unless humans join Earth's revolt, we are not safe either.

This is the wound the angel knows can be healed when he tells Joseph, "[Mary] will bear a son, and you are to name him Jesus, for he will save his people from their sins." However you have heard those words in the past, or hear them presently, it's important that together we understand "save" and "sins," in the way I have explained. This salvation is not an individualistic, psychological saving of souls from this world in anticipation of the next. "Sins" are not primarily about personal morality, but about participating in systems designed by humans that claim to improve on nature's ways. As we see the incredible murder of life that these systems deliver, many of us realize that we've turned away from the call to come out of MultiEarth living. Only by heeding that call and turning to OneEarth ways can we turn from the death-delivering sin by which life is perishing from the Earth. With the perspective of the salvation Jesus so believed in that it finally did him in, we see how to live OneEarth ways. He does, indeed, save his people from their sins. And lest "his people" sound exclusive, let us emphasize say that the angel's wording is about all who make the choice to live in the paradigm which Jesus chose. They are "his people," as the gospels make clear. When we have in mind his creation-centered paradigm, then, when we read the gospels, we see that for Jesus, living interdependently *in* nature is more important than the "progress" that speeds up nature.

If we turn to churches for this healing and salvation, we may well be disappointed. In their many imperial and corporate forms, churches have been ineffective in enacting this kind of healing and salvation. Too many operate too close to the MultiEarth paradigm to call people out of it. As churches evolved historically, they became a civilizing counterforce to the unruly and full salvation in Jesus' name.

Referring again to Wendell Berry, he describes succinctly the results when salvation addresses only the personal and psychological, without applying its transformative energy to the structures, institutions, and powers of society. He observes that in many (even most?) circles calling themselves "Christian," a pernicious dualism exists, counter to the Bible, that separates body and soul, material and spiritual, secular and sacred. Here's how he says it in a collection of essays entitled, *Sex, Economy, Freedom and Community*.

> The modern church presumes to be able to save the soul as an eternal piece of private property. It presumes moreover to save the souls of people in other countries and religion traditions, who are often saner and more religious than we are. And always the emphasis is on the individual soul....
>
> Despite its protests to the contrary, modern Christianity has become willy-nilly the religion of the state and the economic status quo. Because it has been so exclusively dedicated to incanting anemic souls into Heaven, it has been made the tool of much earthly villainy. It has, for the most part, stood silently by while a predatory economy has ravaged the world, destroyed its natural beauty and health, divided and plundered its human communities and households. It has flown the flag and chanted the slogans of empire. . . .
>
> But in its de facto alliance with Caesar, Christianity connives directly in the murder of Creation. For in these days, Caesar is no longer a mere destroyer of armies, cities, and nations. He is a contradictor of the fundamental miracle of life. A part of the normal practice of his power is his willingness to destroy the world. He prays, he says, and churches

everywhere compliantly pray with him. But he is praying to a God whose works he is prepared at any moment to destroy. What could be more wicked than that, or more mad?[16]

But in the creation-centered paradigm where Matthew and Luke operate, the name *Jesus* speaks to healing the wound of dualism and the structural sins left untouched by churches infected with the dualism that pervades MultiEarth civilization.

Immanuel: Divine Presence in All Things and All Interactivity

When Matthew and Luke tell us in their own ways about the moment in which the angel said the newborn would be named Jesus, Matthew inserted another naming moment from an earlier story familiar to him and many Jews. It happened over 700 years before the birth of Jesus when the prophet Isaiah advised Ahaz, King of Judah, not to form alliances with the Empire of Assyria. Given that Ahaz was strongly inclined to do that very thing, Isaiah had to pull out all the stops to make a convincing argument. He said that God was giving Ahaz a sign to assure him that making the Empire of Assyria his ally was not God's way. The sign was that a young woman was to bear a son whom Isaiah named Immanuel, meaning "God with us." With this name, Isaiah sought to strengthen his argument that God's Presence resisted empires. Any alliance with an empire restricted the power of God's Presence. (Isaiah 7:14).

This episode popped into Matthew's memory as he made his case that Mary's womb was filled with God's Presence despite how her relationship with Joseph didn't fit the rules of the Temple and Jewish

---

16 Berry, Wendell. *Sex, Economy, Freedom & Community* (New York: Pantheon Books, 1993), 114-115.

society. When the angel told Joseph in his dream to go ahead and enter into marriage with Mary, Matthew recognized that it was an Immanuel moment.

> "All this took place," Matthew wrote, "to fulfill what had
> been spoken by the Lord through the prophet: 'Look, the
> virgin (or young woman) shall conceive and bear a son, and
> they shall name him Emmanuel,' which means, 'God is with
> us'" (Matthew 1:23).

Matthew's inclusion of the "God with us" name, carries special importance for us in the ecological disasters threatening millions of living things. "God with us" is strongly non-dualistic. Any conceived separation between Creator and creation evaporates. It also goes beyond the widespread idea that the Divine Presence was incarnated in Jesus, but not in anything else. It speaks, rather, of the sacred Presence in all things—something difficult to remember and act on when we feel the injustices and uncaring of debt, difficult or predatory people, inequitable wealth distribution, and the trashing of creation. "God with us" re-ignites the fuel in our souls to imagine again as possible what had become a withered, distant hope. It declares that God's Presence cannot be contained within the order of empires and temples. There is an untamed wildness, an unruliness, to Immanuel that breaks out of the egoistic mind and civilization's ways.

A huge mistake happened in Christianity when, instead of "God with us," creation and Creator were separated. Such dualism lives in the deep wound of our separation from the Earth. When Christianity speaks of "God with us," and refers only to Jesus, not other humans and all creation, it sends tremors through the rest of creation. Without being regarded as embodying the Divine Presence, creation is viewed as spiritless, soul-less—fair game for whatever kind of abuse, extraction, and pillage that serves the interests of growth economics and controllers of power.

In contrast, when "Christianity" came from Europe to the indigenous peoples inhabiting the Americas, the invaders found people who did not think in such dualistic ways about creation and Creator. Pilulaw Khus, a contemporary Chumash woman of California, speaks of the recognition of the Life Force in all things.

> So there were many ways that our people lived that demonstrated the recognition of Life Force, the need for respect, and the interconnection and interaction of all life forms. We were not good "stewards" of the land because nobody stood in that kind of position. We recognize that we are *all* part of Creation and we *all* carry Life Force.
>
> The conquerors considered Indigenous people as not truly human. We were not regarded on the same level of humanness as the conquerors held themselves to be. They called themselves "the people of Reason," and yet they were the ones who were willing to come and impose this exceptional brutality and viciousness onto the people of this land. That was a Holocaust. It was a Holocaust that came down in a very brief time. Chumash People's whole world was destroyed.... If you can imagine your whole world being destroyed, where would your fire for life come from? [17]

The tragedies implemented when dualisms infuse and distort a worldview fade away when cosmology, mystical understandings, and greater

---

17 Broyles-Gonzalez and Pilulaw Khus, *Earth Wisdom: A California Chumash Woman* (Tucson: University of Arizona Press, 2011), 61-64

consciousness of soul shapes the lifeway. The dualism separating creation or creature from Creator is not only foreign to indigenous peoples, it was not and is not true of mystical and Earth spiritualities generally. Mechtild of Magdeberg, a 13th-century mystic of the German Rhineland, testifies to the great change that happened for her when she shifted out of dualistic thinking. Are heaven and earth separate? Not for Mechtild. They are regions of one universe. God is both transcendent and imminent. Mechtild's experience of God exemplifies a vibrant panentheism, which emphasizes both God in us and us in God. Panentheism gives us a unifying alternative, different from and beyond theism, which emphasizes transcendence, and pantheism, which emphasizes immanence. Keenly aware of the damage done *to* people and *by* people practicing dualism, Mechtild criticized clergy for being dualists who stood between people and God rather than facilitating a direct, immediate experience of God. She said, "The day of my spiritual awakening was the day I saw, and knew that I saw, God in all things and all things in God."[18]

Episcopal priest and theologian Matthew Fox, who quotes Mechtild, goes on to say that "panentheism is a way of seeing the world sacramentally."[19] All things and processes embody the Divine Presence—what Pilulaw Khus calls Life Force. The name *Immanuel* speaks of this panentheistic, unifying worldview for OneEarth living today.

---

18 Fox, Matthew. *Original Blessing: A Primer in Creation Spirituality* (Santa Fe, New Mexico: Bear and Company), 88.

19 Ibid, 90.

Savior, Christ the Lord: Soul-Consciousness for a New Creation

When the angel startles the shepherds into a cosmological experience, he says, "Unto you is born this day in the city of David, a Savior, who is Christ, the Lord." The angel gives no other name to the newborn. He only explains that they'll find a baby wrapped in the cloths common to peasant parents and lying in the manger of a peasant home. I've already described the importance of Savior, but here the angel explains that this Savior is "Christ, the Lord." This explicit connection of Jesus to Christ, or Messiah, adds to what I've already pointed out—how Messiah (Christ) is being reinterpreted in the birth stories of Matthew and Luke. They take the controversial step in their birth stories, and throughout their gospels, of moving the significance of Messiah away from the narrow political meaning of reinstating the monarchy begun by David.

Matthew and Luke picked up on another strand in the meaning of Messiah that emphasizes a consciousness greater than the rebirth of political monarchy. This strand of Messianism makes imperial thinking obsolete and turns instead to how divine consciousness transcends the complex of powers that comprise empires. This kind of Messianism empowers a reign that, unlike empires, never ends. It is a consciousness of which our souls are fully capable, a consciousness that perceives and participates in the Great Mystery. From within that mystery comes a constant regeneration of our humanity. It is the source of a new story of origins, a new story of creation. As we join with Jesus and all who learn to move beyond egoistic living into living from the center of our souls, we access the greater divine consciousness that shapes the structures of life in the new creation.

I continue to contrast the story of origins that gives birth to the new creation with the story of origins that rules the world today. The latter's origins arise with the story of civilization. It ignores completely the First Peoples globally who have lived by more primordial stories of origins that predate civilization. Adherents of the civilization project live with an assumption that their creation story is far better and supplants the creation stories of First Peoples and any story of OneEarth creation. Creation stories of First Peoples illustrate a rich cosmology, as do the first chapters of Genesis and the unruly birth stories of Jesus. Cosmology, as already stated, dwarfs history while including it. Cosmology is wildly free compared to civilization's ways directed by egos and their controlling consciousness. In soul consciousness, where we resonate with cosmology, we humans participate in the ways of the new creation and exemplify that to be truly human differs radically from the greedy, power-hungry, violence-inclined people that civilization says we are.

Let me say it one more time. Civilization expresses ego consciousness, not soul consciousness. Soul consciousness lives by a different creation story and shapes a world of right relationships and sharing. Humans live within the Earth's community of life—not ruling over it; not even stewarding it, but discovering what it means to be human *within* Earth's interdependent, relational abundance.

Being *within* Earth's community of life also makes important the angel's use of "Lord." The full phrase is "Christ, the Lord." Throughout this book, I've continually referred to *Christ* as the name for divine consciousness rather than a particular individual. It has been especially connected to Jesus because of his clear embodiment of that consciousness. He was called *Jesus the Christ,* or simply *Jesus Christ.* To add *Lord* as a title is an unmistakable confrontation with the political slogan, "Caesar is Lord," a common slogan of loyalty throughout the Roman Empire. To call anyone else *Lord* defied Caesar's status and called attention to one's disloyalty. Followers of the Way of Jesus, however, found it difficult to use the political slogan. It stuck in their throats. They knew that Jesus, by contrast, deserved the title because the divine consciousness with which he lived was greater than the egoistic consciousness of the emperor. Though empires and nations have lords that rule, in the new creation story "the Lord" refers to the overriding consciousness of the divine that outlaws imperial lords. Clearly, the angel did not make life easier for the followers of Jesus by giving him the title *Lord*.

So it is that "a Savior who is Christ, the Lord" means one conceived and nourished in soul consciousness. One who in his life and death heals the tragic breaches created by dualisms—the wounds of humanity, the Earth, and all of life, by which we have been torn from the humus that is our essence. Just think of all the divisions driven by the structures created by MultiEarth thinking that keep humans subordinate, separated, and severed from our souls. This soul consciousness, or Christ consciousness, can heal the deep, tearing wounds of civilization. Especially important in this moment is that, wherever it is embodied, it can reverse climate change and other devastating ecological impacts of MultiEarth living. Such is the consciousness liberated by the wild birth of Jesus, untamed by Christmas, that empowers the ways of living urged by the new creation story.

CHAPTER SEVEN
Being Part of the New Creation Now

Living the New Creation Story Ourselves

To sum up, and perhaps add a few thoughts, I want to emphasize that we have the capacities to live the new creation story ourselves. In this time, we need to liberate the creation story of 587 B.C.E. (Genesis) and the creation story of 85 C.E. (the gospels) from the civilization story so that their full voltage can empower us to reverse the ecological catastrophes we see unfolding. The false creation story, which is actually a destruction story, told by the industrial-military-technological worldview of how civilization began 12,000 years ago has captured countless minds and provided a compelling way to live prosperously—though prosperity is for only a minority, and at the expense of the Earth. As we now see clearly, the story of the origins of civilization is a MultiEarth story, not a survival story, but a story resulting in the death of life. In the 21st century, this imperial MultiEarth story is embodied in the global corporations and their vassal nation-states, led by the United States and a handful of others with huge economies. Compellingly decorated with endlessly new, shiny technologies, their story now rules primarily for the benefit of 1 percent the Earth's 7.5 billion and counting. As they ravage the biosphere and planet in search of cheap, extractable resources, they bypass locals and their economies, and then dump toxic waste faster than the Earth can digest it. How can these runaway horses of the apocalypse be reined in? As Matthew and Luke show, it takes a cosmological story of a new creation. Only such a story can checkmate the corporate story.

For such a story to press forward among all who identify as Christian—as well as all others who lean toward that path or learn from it, and all who do not see themselves as religious at all—it's vital to remember that Jesus was born in Bethlehem, within time, in a particular place; but Christ, whether one thinks of such a spirit as conceptual or metaphysical, was and is from the beginning. As John says in his gospel—one that would come after the ones written by Matthew and Luke—"In the beginning was the Logos," or Word or Life Force or Christ. To say, "Christ was born in Bethlehem," is a theological affirmation, not a historical statement. My point here is that using Jesus and Christ interchangeably, without awareness of how they have separate lineages and definitions, fuzzes over important distinctions necessary for the compelling story of the new creation our current crises call for. With the loss of those distinctions, the Christ of the cosmos gets reduced to the proportions of history—a serious mistake, and never more so than when we are up against the massive extinctions and ecological catastrophe well underway.

It's helpful to understand how in the gospels and epistles we see the creativity of people 20 centuries ago connecting the Jesus of Bethlehem and the Christ of the eons and cosmos. Their context, however, differs from ours in that *"Christ" was not then assumed to be Jesus' second name. What is especially important for us today is to rediscover how they are separate.* Only then can we rediscover a healthy, connecting relationship between them, instead of the co-dependent, dysfunctional linking that fails us when we need a big, cosmic-proportioned story with which to deal with our contemporary ecological, economic, and cultural realities. The previous chapters have opened the door to such further pondering of the mystery contained in the distinction and the relationship between Jesus (of history) and Christ (of the cosmos).

I want to remind us how reluctantly Jesus called himself Christ or Messiah. Jesus preferred other designations, his favorite being "the human one" or "the truly human one," a translation that says more than "Son of Man," which is used in many versions of the Bible. To recognize the way of Jesus as truly human emphasizes the treasure and power of being human in the ways of a greater consciousness than what ego-controlled, profit-driven living can bring forth.

Given how wary Jesus was to identify himself with much of the Messianic mythology that developed in several strands over centuries before his life, we do well to ask why many, soon after his life and ever since, have so readily called Jesus "Christ." For Jesus, lots of the Messianic mythology was filled with expectations that would subvert him from his divine call, rather than fulfill it. This was especially true of the politicized stories of Christ as one who would seek political control. *He also feared the outcome of Messianism that projected powers onto him that we humans need to own for ourselves. Jesus' way was for everyone to incarnate Christ as he did.* Why else did he say referring to his works that left people amazed, "You will do greater things than these" (John 14:12).

Just as the gospel writers understood "Jesus was born in Bethlehem" as a historical statement, they understood that the origins of Christ were cosmological, from the beginning of time. Whether or not we can relate to Christ as cosmological—as Divine Mind, Presence, Spirit, or consciousness embodied in human history and in all of creation—depends on our willingness to get beyond our egos and pursue a greater consciousness ourselves. A consciousness needing a rationally ordered world and recognizing that truth can only be held in historical fact will of necessity reduce Christ to the size of mere reason or history—something Jesus shunned. A common way so to reduce Christ is to equate the Christ with Jesus unreflectively and give it no further thought.

It's also far too common to connect cosmo-centric knowing, wisdom, and power exclusively with Jesus while keeping it out of reach of humanity. This defeats exactly what Jesus sought to do, which was to see Christ in a fuller incarnation throughout creation. When the angel urged the shepherds to see, it was the opening fanfare to the life of Jesus, a highly energized focus on healing our blindness to the Christ power spread throughout creation since the beginning. Jesus continued to emphasize "opening eyes" and "opening ears." Both are graphic metaphors for the blindness and deafness of a consciousness unable to perceive that the Christ is available to all and in all. This understanding of consciousness, one whose time across the Earth, changes the MultiEarth worldview now killing life in the oceans, on the land, and in the air. When this soul consciousness incarnates in us, whether it's called Christ consciousness or a name given it by other religions and cultures, then we become eager to configure our lives within the unfolding new creation story.

I hope that however you describe and know the relationship between such consciousness and all creation, that it is a relationship too numinous ever to be captured by words at all, let alone a single set of verbal symbols. That relationship is essential to the transforming adventure in the new creation. There is no formula or arrangement of words that can ever encapsulate the interrelationships and interactions involved. I am well aware that certain arrangements of words have pleased some who proceed to make them orthodox or *the* correct way to talk about what must, if truth is our concern, always remain a mystery and beyond verbal arrangements. So, the importance of my words is not that I have said it "correctly," but that I am testifying to my experience of how the interrelationship of the consciousness of our most soulful ways with the Divine Presence continues to be transformative. It continues to give me goose bumps. It continues to reconfigure what I think I know. The interrelationships I sense continue to take me into conversations and awesome places where my rational mind knows that I can utter no more words. Perhaps I am most a part of right relationships when I become silent in the presence of the sacred. There are times when my heart takes off its shoes, and whispers, *Holy*.

We *do* have the capacity to live Mary's song of economic equality with all creation, as well as the cosmos' angels words of living in peace without fear. Claiming these capacities of soul consciousness and the spreading of Christ in all things and processes reverses ecological catastrophe with the powers of the new creation. It's part of life in the OneEarth worldview where the powers of the cosmos are not separate, but one with us.

Standing with Mother Earth and All Life Inside the New Creation Story

Within the pages of this book are many actions for shaping life in the story of the new creation. The following are examples of standing with the Earth, our planetary Mother, and all beings.

1. *Replacing patriarchy*—Standing with Tamar and women and men who are replacing patriarchy. Without a release of the Feminine, humanity does not have the energies necessary to make the enormous shift from living according to the

MultiEarth story to living within OneEarth's new creation story.

2. *Loving our adversaries*—Standing with Rahab and all who are intent on loving our enemies. Dualistic thinking requires enemies. The thinking that goes with panentheism dissolves dualisms. All who were enemies to one another must become partners in a larger consciousness that embraces all in the larger story of the new creation.

3. *Advocating for immigrants*—Standing with Ruth and all who advocate for immigrants. It means recognizing that we are all immigrants, or descended from them. It means seeing that Judaism was likely a religion formed of various refugees and migrants. It means seeing that the early Jesus movement was especially composed of many marginal peasants clinging to their land or already pushed off of it by war, fraud, or commercialism in which they could not compete. Landowners and people of positions were few in the early movement. Immigrant advocacy constantly challenges the meaning of borders and who gets to define them. The work of immigrants and their advocates is prophetic, pointing to the need for a world order led by people not limited to ego consciousness. At the moment we have borders that can be easily crossed by currencies, economies, and transnational corporations, but not by people. Living the story of the new creation requires reimagining an arrangement beyond nation-states that use their power to control and restrict rather than to exchange the riches of life's diversity.

4. *Exposing modern empire complexes*—Standing with Bathsheba in exposing the empire from within requires learning to stand in truth and love no matter how powerful the imperial

corporations or personalities we face. The difficulties of this cannot be exaggerated, nor, because of its importance, can this action be left to others.

5. *Economics of redistribution*—Standing with Mary in the economics of redistribution challenges today's versions of growth economics and the laws that continually redistribute wealth from those with less to those with more. The moral and economic issue is not redistribution itself. The issue is the direction of the redistribution. Those who self-righteously argue against redistribution downward, claim that redistribution itself is non-capitalist and wrong. But they are not perturbed by the moral issues of redistribution upward. MultiEarth powers practice redistribution upward; the new creation story practices redistribution downward and outward in ways practiced throughout creation.

6. *Panentheism*—Standing with all who see the Divine Presence in all things and all interactions (panentheism). Practicing this spiritual path, whatever one's religion or ethical tradition, heals the wound of separation from creation and moves us into living the new creation story.

7. *Healing separation from the soil*—Standing with all who by their actions heal the tearing wound of separation from the Earth. Organic and regenerative farmers connect with the soil and work to make it healthy. Their focus is on increasing organisms in it. From there, nutritious food will grow. Also, working soil ourselves in order to grow food heals us. Eating as a high a percentage of organic food as possible contributes greatly to healing this deep wound.

8. *Racism*—Standing with Rahab and Ruth and all who challenge separatist, exclusionary treatment based on ethnicity

and race. Despite people who claim to be non-racist, it is not possible to be completely free of the deep phobias that divide us according to this social plague. We can, however, be against racism. Living the new creation story moves beyond dividing by race, recognizing how much differences contribute to the rich wholeness of creation's interdependent community of life.

9. *Significance of dreams*—Standing with Joseph and the magi who made major life decisions based on information that came to them from their unconscious self via their dream-maker. Ego consciousness discounts the unconscious as a means of dealing with its deep fear of what lives there. Soul consciousness welcomes new material from the unconscious for the potentials, directions, and energies that come into our lives from the dream world. Our souls recognize dreams as the language of God.

10. *Moving beyond dualisms*—Standing with all who challenge the dualistic thinking of ego consciousness that divides, separates, isolates, and cuts us off in wounded and wounding ways. Beyond merely challenging this dualism, in soul consciousness, we can think and act in new ways in which dualisms become two poles in a greater whole. The interaction of the poles creates essential energies for transformation in the ways necessary for the new creation.

11. *Incorporate cosmology into our lives.*—Cosmology incorporates science with other forms of knowing. It opens us to (1) our unconscious knowing, some of which surfaces in our dreams, and some surfaces in waking imagery and intuitions we have about benevolent or malevolent people, places, and events; (2) the recognition that plants, our planet, and other

species have forms of consciousness and communicate with other members of the biosphere, including us; and (3) seeing the various forms in which the ancestors are present in our lives and can offer guidance. Without deepening our understanding of cosmology we cut ourselves off from a major source of energy and knowing. By our actions we need to affirm that cosmology is essential in order for a OneEarth worldview to be strong enough to make MultiEarth ways obsolete.

Related Readings

Berry, Wendell. *The Hidden Wound,* (New York: North Point Press), 1989

Broyles-Gonzalez, Yolanda and Pilulaw Khus. *Earth Wisdom: A California Chumash Woman* (Tucson: The University of Arizona Press), 2011

Eisler, Riane. *The Real Wealth of Nations: Creating a Caring Economics* (Oakland, California: Berrett-Koehler Publishers), 2007

Fox, Matthew. *The Coming of the Cosmic Christ* (New York: HarperCollins Publishers), 1988

Fox, Matthew. *Original Blessing: A Primer in Creation* Spirituality (Santa Fe, New Mexico: Bear and Company), 1983

Howard-Brook, Wes. *Come Out My People: God's Call Out of Empire in the Bible and Beyond* (Maryknoll, New York: Orbis Books), 2010

Howard-Brook, Wes. *Empire Baptized: How the Church Embraced What Jesus Rejected* (Maryknoll, New York: Orbis Books), 2016

Kelsey, Morton. *Dreams: A Way to Listen to God* (New York: Paulist Press), 1978

Kimmerer, Robin Wall. *Braided Sweetgrass: Indigenous Wisdom, Scientific Knowledge, and the Teachings of Plants* (Minneapolis: Milkweed Editions), 2013

Metzger, Bruce and Michael Coogan (eds.). *The Oxford Companion to the Bible* (Oxford: Oxford University Press), 1993

Ringe, Sharon and Wes Howard-Brook (ed). *The New Testament— Introducing the Way of Discipleship* (Maryknoll, New York: Orbis Books), 2002

Van Ham, Lee. *Blinded by Progress: Breaking Out of the Illusion that Holds Us* (San Diego: OneEarth Publishing), 2013

Van Ham, Lee. From Egos to Eden: Our Heroic Journey to Keep Earth Livable (San Diego: OneEarth Publishing), 2016

Gratitude

EVERY BOOK I WRITE TAKES me for a walk in a field of gratitude. As I was writing these pages I was often surprised by what I wrote. "Where did these thoughts come from?" I would ask. My muse was always with me. She worked with what I've learned from more people, books, articles, and experiences than I can remember. All of these continually congeal in me in various ways to stir imagination and intuition that generate personal insights that excite me. So I write them. Days later I rewrite them. I ask others to read what I've been rewriting, and their thoughts contribute to more rewriting and to what is here published. From among the many who are part of this book, let me call out the following in particular.

Jerry Iversen, director of Simple Living Works, was the first to plant the seed in me that the blogs I'd been writing about Christmas could be the core of an important book. He'd already included the blogs in his annual Christmastime release, "Whose Birthday Is It Anyway?" Still, I didn't have the gut feeling or passion to do the work of writing a book. That changed during Christmas 2018. It was a good holiday for me. I enjoyed the family relationships and loved the magical tree in our living room. But I realized that the transforming powers in the story of the birth of Jesus were barely a part of what I experienced. And, I felt that what was happening in the world ecologically and politically needed those powers. Christmas, as such, was a retreat from engagement with the larger world, and once the season passed, so did the opportunity to expose ourselves to the energies of the cosmos that are inherent in this story of a new humanity, a new creation, and a new consciousness able to engage the extinctions of life underway in apocalyptic dimensions. I asked Jerry to be the first reader when I completed a manuscript. He quickly obliged and made many suggestions. I incorporated most of them.

Grace Gyori responded to my request that she write a "Foreword" to the book. Grace's early years were in China where her parents were missionaries in the imperial way that Christian missions typically proceeded then. After marrying Tom, the two went to Guatemala and discovered a new paradigm for mission work in which they were radicalized regarding U.S. imperialism as they worked with the people in a model of sharing work led by local leaders. I'm grateful to Grace for recalling experiences we've shared and weaving them into her valuable "Foreword."

Charlie Flowerday and I had been absent from one another's lives for maybe 40 years when we exchanged a few messages on Facebook in the past year. In those messages I learned that he did editing. When I asked if he would edit my manuscript, we were mutually excited by the thought. Phew! Edit it he did. He worked fervently and it took me days to rework the manuscript to consider all of his important changes. I'm grateful for his work, and that it rekindled our relationship. I also wish him success with some manuscripts which he's written and are worthy of publication.

As I asked people to read my pre-published manuscript and write a blurb or endorsement of it, I wondered who would be able to do so. Not everyone I asked could do it for one reason or another, but most agreed. Then, when they agreed, I wondered, "What will they write?

How will the book strike them?" Those questions are answered in the pages "What Other People Say about This Book." I urge you to read their thoughts. Each one has an important perspective to share. I will not name them all again here, but I do express gratitude to each of them … and promise to send them a free copy before Christmas this year.

This book was taken from manuscript to both eBook and print copy through the skills of David Wogahn, head of Authorimprints. I've worked with David on each of my books. His integrity in every aspect of the publishing process—creating a cover, formatting the manuscript, arranging for print-on-demand publishing, getting it posted for sale, pricing, and more—brings great relief to me. He works with me step by step to achieve an attractive book. David is a strong advocate for authors and really wants each book to reach its audience. I'm deeply grateful for how he's worked with me to create this book and encourages me in the work of marketing.

The footnotes and the books under the heading, "Related Reading," have been teachers to me. The formality of the footnotes and "Related Reading" hide the emotion and spirit that each holds. For each one, I am grateful for all the work that went into writing these and then sharing them with whoever choose to read.

Finally, great thanks to Jubilee Economics Ministries for the up-front funding of this book. A nonprofit with Circles in Mexico and San Diego, OneEarth Jubilee Economics has inspired me for the past 20 years with its vision and practice. It would be special if the royalties would repay that investment. Without the investment, this book would not have become available.

Index

Made in the USA
Lexington, KY
22 November 2019